THE DAMNED

VOLUME 2, "ILL-GOTTEN"

THE DAM

INED™

VOLUME 2, "ILL-GOTTEN"

Written by
CULLEN BUNN

Illustrated by
BRIAN HURTT

Colored by
BILL CRABTREE

Lettered by
CRANK!

Designed by
KEITH WOOD

Edited by
DESIREE WILSON with **CHARLIE CHU**

AN ONI PRESS PUBLICATION

THE DAMNED: "ILL-GOTTEN"
BY CULLEN BUNN, BRIAN HURTT, & BILL CRABTREE

Published by Oni Press, Inc.
Joe Nozemack, founder & chief financial officer
James Lucas Jones, publisher
Charlie Chu, v.p. of creative & business development
Brad Rooks, director of operations
Rachel Reed, marketing manager
Melissa Meszaros, publicity manager
Troy Look, director of design & production
Hilary Thompson, senior graphic designer
Kate Z. Stone, junior graphic designer
Angie Knowles, digital prepress lead
Ari Yarwood, executive editor
Robin Herrera, senior editor
Desiree Wilson, associate editor
Alissa Sallah, administrative assistant
Jung Lee, logistics associate

Oni Press, Inc
1319 SE Martin Luther King, Jr. Blvd
Suite 240
Portland, OR 97214

onipress.com
facebook.com/onipress · twitter.com/onipress
onipress.tumblr.com · instagram.com/onipress

cullenbunn.com · @cullenbunn
brihurtt.com · @brihurtt
@crabtree_bill
@ccrank

First edition: April 2018
ISBN 978-1-62010-485-9
eISBN 978-1-62010-486-6

Library of Congress Control Number: 2016951885

10 9 8 7 6 5 4 3 2 1

Printed in China

CHAPTER

1

Gangsters grow rich on our vices, and rivalries between criminal organizations result in bloody massacres in the streets. But unknown to the masses, demonic families control the rackets, using greed, gluttony, lust and other sins to fuel a lucrative trade: mortal souls.

Eddie's soul was forfeit long ago, and he's been cursed for his trouble. The best he can do is avoid a city that seems to want him dead—and frequently succeeds—just so he can crawl right back out of the gutter, alive and kicking at the expense of some unfortunate mortal who dared touch him. Thanks to recent dirty dealings of his own, Eddie's found himself in charge of the Gehenna Room, a posh club with one rule: no demons allowed.

Now, a friend from Eddie's past has arrived, seeking sanctuary from the demonic forces pursing him. Pauly Bones, a friend from Eddie's past arrives at the club, seeking sanctuary from the demonic forces pursuing him, and Eddie knows nothing good can come of it. Pauly Bones always has a few ulterior motives and this is no different. This time, he wants Eddie to help him free a few souls from the infernal, including the soul of the cursed, beautiful Deidra.

Eddie – The owner of the Gehenna Room.

Pauly Bones – An old friend of Eddie's. A gambler whose luck seems to have taken a turn.

Deidra – Pauly's old flame, now horribly cursed.

The Aligheri Family – The most powerful demon family in the city.

The Roarke Family – The second strongest demon family, and none too happy about it.

The Verlochin – An exiled demon brood that adheres to the ancient infernal ways.

This town's got more than its share of grifters, skid rogues, and hatchet men.

I ought to know.

I count myself amongst them.

Move!

Move!

But I'm the only one who ends up with his throat *cut wide* on the *regular*.

Out of the way!

It's almost a joke among a certain class of scum.

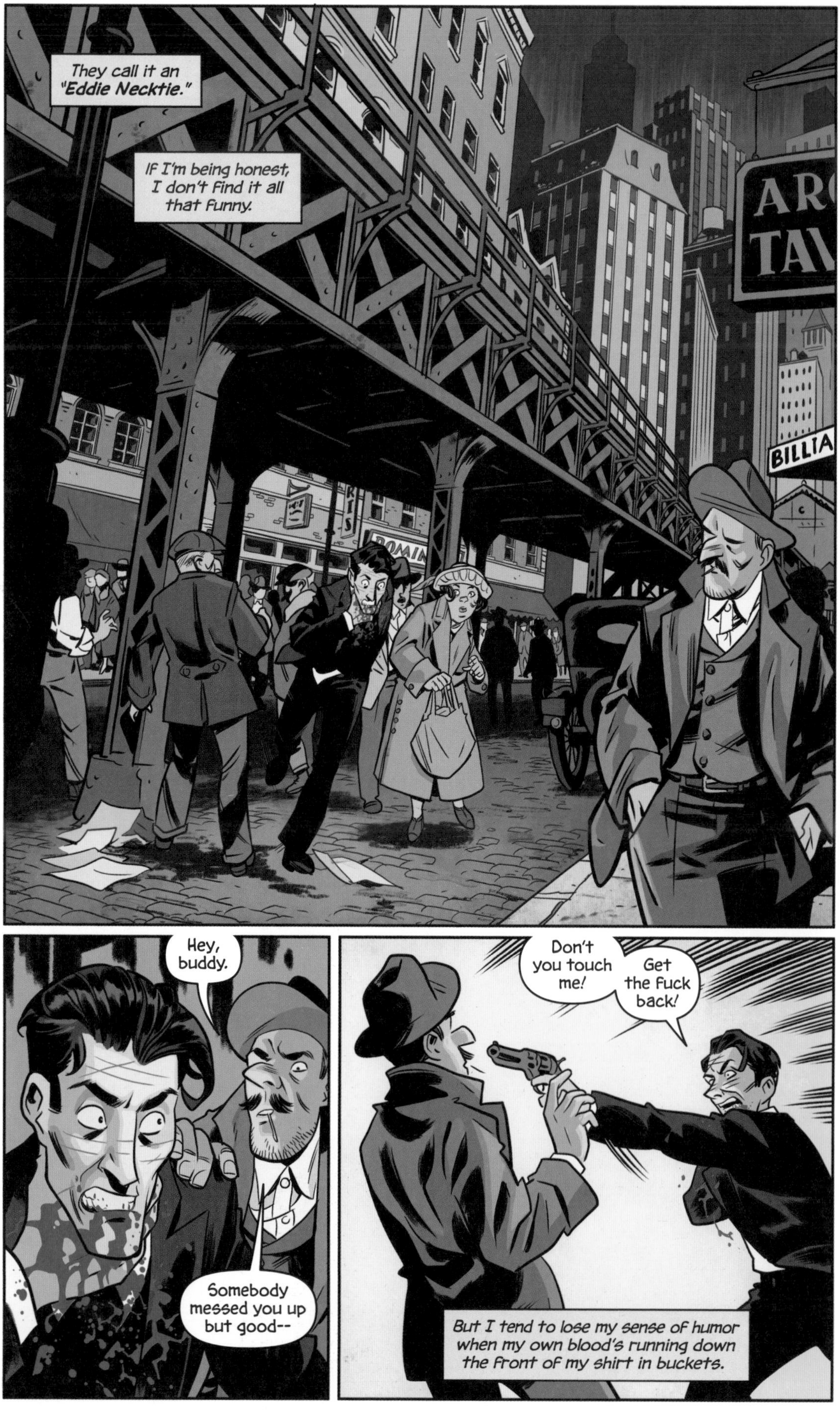
They call it an "Eddie Necktie."
If I'm being honest, I don't find it all that funny.
Hey, buddy.
Somebody messed you up but good--
Don't you touch me!
Get the fuck back!
But I tend to lose my sense of humor when my own blood's running down the front of my shirt in buckets.

But here's the **real** gas.

Get lost, ya bum!

I might die... in fact, I **probably** will.

But I probably won't stay that way.

That's my **curse**.

But that's only **part** of it.

Because in order for me to come back from the hereafter, someone else has to take my place.

After I'm done breathing, anyone who touches my corpse goes **tits up**, while I'm on my feet again.

That's one of the reasons I try to limit my activities to specific **social circles**.

When I'm outside my element, innocent people tend to get hurt.

I do what I can to keep the **collateral damage** to a minimum, but like I said...

...I'm just one of many sons of bitches who call this city home.

24 Hours Earlier.

Place is really hopping tonight, Mr. Tamblyn!

It's just... just something else!

Hey, Ricky...

...how about getting my friends here a couple of drinks on the house?

Yes, sir!

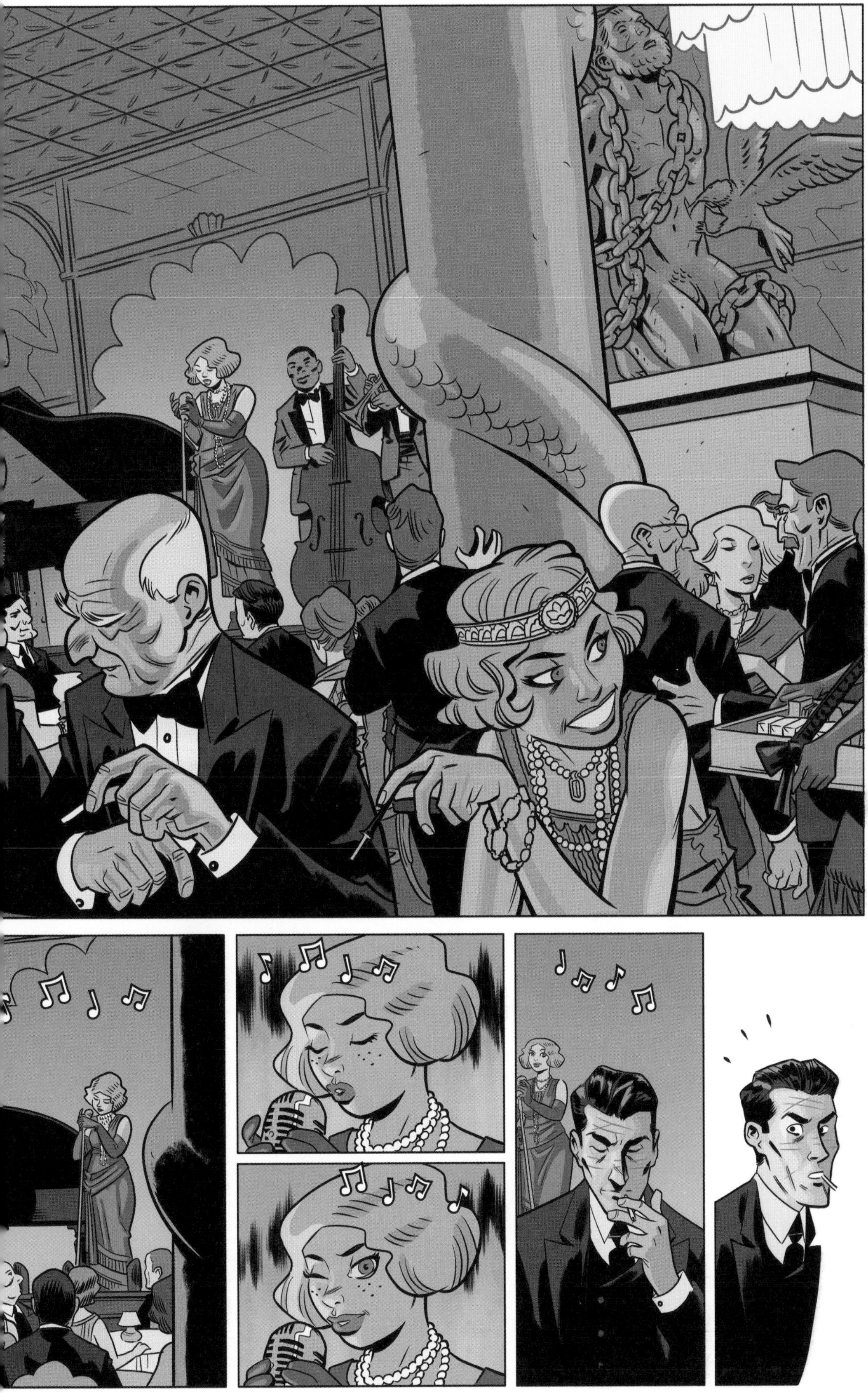

Can I help you gents?

Naw, naw.

Me and my mates here just thought we'd check out the ol' stomping grounds, y'know?

Have a few *drinks*, a few *laughs*.

Maybe you should look elsewhere.

Maybe you haven't heard, but the Gehenna Room's gone *exclusive*.

No demons allowed.

Now that ya mention it, I *did* hear something about that.

Thought it sounded like something might be *bad fer business*.

An' I thought you could make an *exception* if the mood struck ya.

I don't see my mood changing anytime soon.

So you can take your crew and drift.

C'mon, Eddie.

I mean--look-- the average soul in this place is so *lily white*, won't none of your customers know the difference.

They'll never know there are demons amongst 'em.

I'll know.

Well, yeah, you'd know.

Yer one of *the damned*, Eddie, so yer eyes don't hide the *awfulness* from ya.

Yer an original *rule-breaker*, which is how I know you can look the other way as we shuffle on past, right?

Not hardly.

Time to shove off, fellas.

These guys might say they're just here for a good time, but demons have a way of talking out of the sides of their necks.

They're looking for someone.

13

The questions are:

Who?

And how bad am I getting screwed without even knowing it?

You know what, Eddie... this is yer place. Yer the *boss*.

Who am I to tell ya if ya know yer onions or not?

We'll *dangle* if that's how you like it.

But you should think about what's good fer yer *wellbeing... financial* an' *otherwise*.

It's not a smart businessman who turns paying customers away at the door.

I'm *not* a businessman.

I'm just lucky enough to own a club where demons aren't allowed.

Yer rules, Eddie.

Yer *funeral*.

Demons... Bruno Roarke's *hatchetmen*... in my club.

Members of that family wouldn't but rarely be found in the Gehenna Room even when the place was under old-fashioned management.

Whoever those party crashers were looking for, they didn't spot them.

Or maybe they did.

You know what's good about a bunch of horn-headed, cloven Foot types showing up at your doorstep?

Nothing.

It's all just varying degrees of bad.

When any one of the demon families takes an interest in your affairs, there's only one thing you can bank on.

And that's *trouble*.

Best to find it...

...before *it* Finds you.

What do you say, ladies and gentlemen?

How about a big round of applause for the musical stylings of *Darcy Lang!*

15

Beautiful, Ms. Lang! Simply lovely!

...voice of an angel...

...wasted in a town like this...

Can I buy you a drink?

So, boss... what did you think?

For a minute there, Darcy, you made me forget how heavy the world is on my shoulders.

Aw.

Isn't that just the *sweetest thing?*

I hope you remember that sweetness...

...when it comes time to *renegotiate* my *contract.*

Managing the Gehenna Room...

...*hobnobbing* with the rich and powerful...

...discussing *contract negotiations*...

If I didn't know any better, Eddie...

...I'd think you had grown a set of *horns* yourself.

The Eddie I grew up with wouldn't never *turn demon*, would he?

But that can't be right, can it?

And just like that...

...it all makes a stomach-churning kind of sense.

Pauly Bones.

Doesn't take a whole lot of smarts to see who Bruno Roarke's boys were looking for.

What do you say, Edward?

It's been way too long, yeah?

If I had known, I might have let the demons have the run of the place just long enough to drag him out.

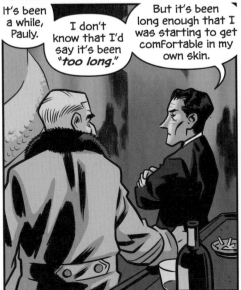

It's been a while, Pauly.

I don't know that I'd say it's been *"too long."*

But it's been long enough that I was starting to get comfortable in my own skin.

From the looks of it, though...

...you haven't been staying in any one place long enough to take root.

Ha! Ain't that the truth?

I *missed* the old gang.

No matter how far and wide you travel, though, you always get the *itch* to come home again.

How's *Sophie?* I was looking, but didn't see her around--

What are you doing here, Pauly? I haven't heard a peep from you in--what is it, now?--Four years.

You show up on my doorstep out of the blue, a couple of scuffed up suitcases next to your over-polished scuffed up shoes...

...I've got to figure this *isn't* just a *social call.*

Yeah, Eduardo, yeah.

When you're right, you're right.

I guess we do have a spot of *business* to discuss, huh?

I've been hearing things, y'know? Hearing how you're a real *fancypants* now.

And I thought maybe you might be in a position--way on up there in your tower--to help an old pal out.

I thought maybe you'd be willing to put me up a few days.

Take a look around, Pauly.

The Gehenna Room's not some *Flophouse.*

We don't just let out rooms to anyone off the street.

Come on, Eddie. Hear me out.

I know you don't let demons in here. That's why I came to you.

I'm not asking for a room.

I'm seeking *sanctuary.*

After all...

...you *owe* me.

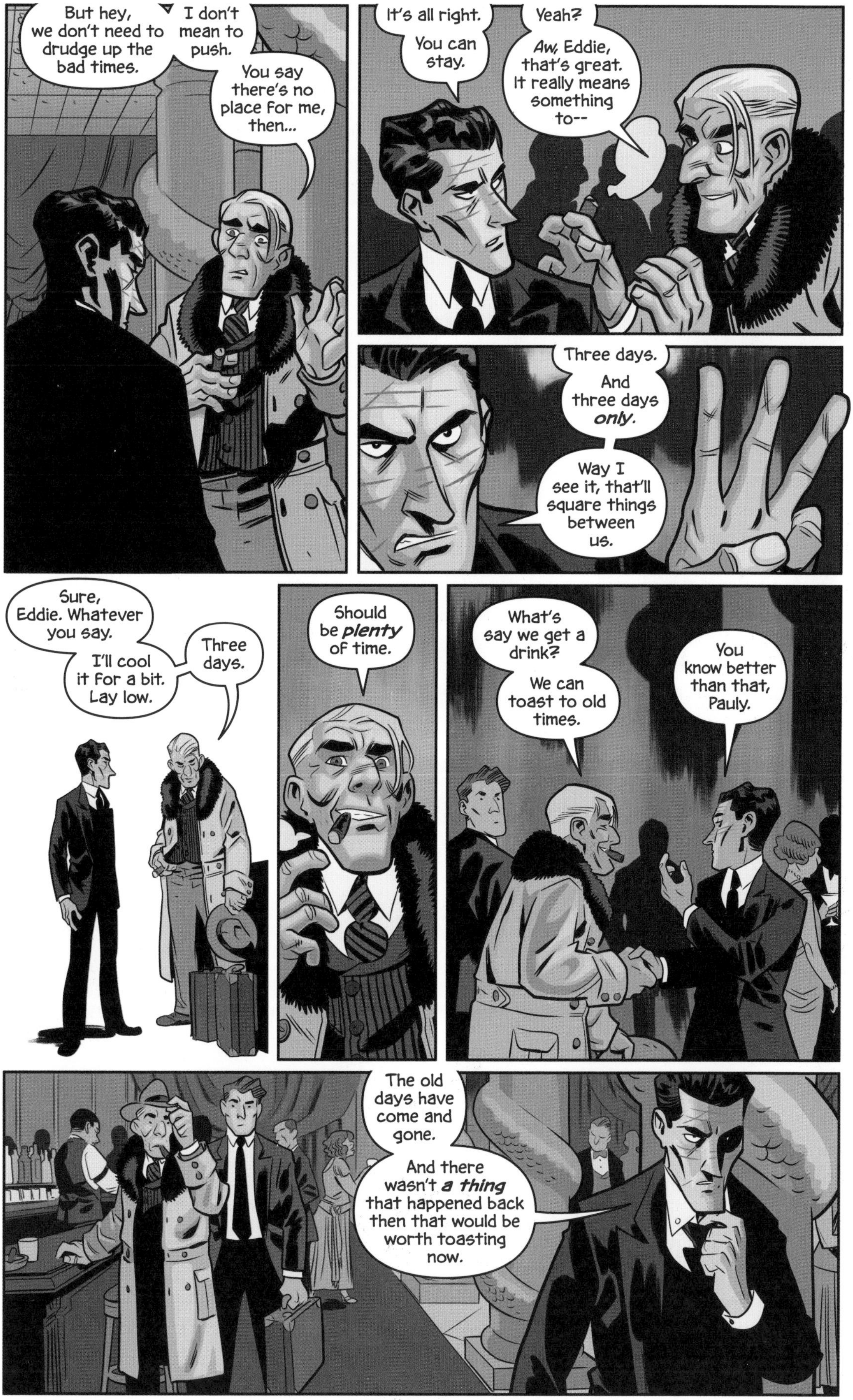
But hey, we don't need to drudge up the bad times.
I don't mean to push.
You say there's no place for me, then...
It's all right.
You can stay.
Yeah?
Aw, Eddie, that's great. It really means something to--
Three days.
And three days only.
Way I see it, that'll square things between us.
Sure, Eddie. Whatever you say.
I'll cool it for a bit. Lay low.
Three days.
Should be plenty of time.
What's say we get a drink?
We can toast to old times.
You know better than that, Pauly.
The old days have come and gone.
And there wasn't a thing that happened back then that would be worth toasting now.

When it comes to *power*, a lot of folks talk about **old money**.

Like being born with a silver spoon up your rear is the same as being born with a crown on your head.

Lemme tell you something about old money.

You dig deep enough, you'll tap the *vein* that bled it out.

All that cash... all that power... almost always came from someplace **dark and bloody**.

It came from someplace mortal... and, for that reason, it don't mean *squat* in the grand scheme of things.

For demons, *souls* are old money.

They've made a brisk trade, using the rackets to get poor bastards to sell their one and only shot of hobbling through the Pearly Gates.

And they bicker and argue over the trade of those souls, same as any deadbeat squabbling over a few bills.

Ask me, they've spent so much time around mortals, they're starting to pick up our *bad habits*.

But *secrets*...

...like the secrets the Serpent whispered from its tree...

...those are the *oldest* currency.

The demon families know this.

That's why they keep their *true faces* hidden from anyone who hasn't signed their bloody name on the dotted line.

And if that doesn't sum up the nature of secrets, I don't know what does.

I'm going out.

You need me to get you a driver?

I'd rather walk.

They're *treacherous*, once they're *uncovered*.

No matter how bright and shiny the truth might be...

...when someone comes your way trafficking in secrets, the smart play is to run the other way.

But I've always been more *curious* than *smart*.

I've got the *scars* to prove it.

KNOK
KNOK

Why, Eddie... as I live and breathe.

Didn't nobody think they'd ever see you in these parts again.

What are you doing here?

Slumming?

Way I heard it, you moved out of your flat and straight into a *room with a view.*

The view's not so *grand* as you might expect.

I miss the old stomping ground from time to time.

Odd, then, that you haven't visited before now.

Rubbing elbows with high rollers must keep you busy.

You know how it goes, Deidra.

I've heard enough of your stories to know that you used to count yourself *among* those high rollers.

Back before either one of us were *cursed*.

Is that why you're here? You want an *etiquette lesson?*

Give it up, Eddie dear, you've embraced your inner lowlife. There's no changing that now.

Lucky for you, I've always had a *weakness* for *reprobates*.

Funny you should mention that.

I wanted to ask you about a guy you used to run with-- *Pauly Bones*.

Why aren't you asking the *Wyrm?*

I thought he kept you well-supplied in *dirty little secrets*.

The Wyrm and me are *quits* these days.

Besides, I figured you've likely been keeping tabs on Ol' Pauly...

...seeing as you two were *close* and all.

Listen to you, choosing your words so *delicately*. Maybe there's a place for you among the *upper crust* after all.

Tea?

No, thanks.

I'm not... thirsty.

No.

I wouldn't expect so.

Deidra, it **is** good to see you again. I mean that.

But if you could help me out, it would mean a lot.

You know what Pauly's been up to lately?

Believe it or not, I stopped caring about Pauly's activities some time ago.

I carried that torch so long it nearly burned my fingers off.

Last I heard, he was rolling dice in **Atlantic City**, taking his chances with a **crueler** class of **fiend**.

Why do you ask?

Have you heard from him? Seen him?

How **unlucky** do you think I am?

Just curious is--

Hsst!

Don't touch me!

Aw, Hell. I'm sorry, Dee.

I just forget sometimes, y'know?

It's all right.

It's kind of sweet, actually, and completely unlike you...

...to forget what we **really** are.

It really is sad that we don't see you more often.

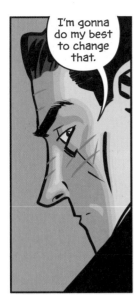

I'm gonna do my best to change that.

Liar.

So Pauly Bones had been traipsing across the boardwalk like a real butter and egg man...

...spending money he likely didn't have, seeing as how he's always on the nut.

Put himself in a real bad fix with the demons.

I guess I know how that feels.

But he's tracking his dirty footprints across *my* carpet now.

The horn-heads figure Pauly and me used to be tight, so they're gonna lean on me to get to him.

They don't care that the water under that bridge is as *bloody* as--

Hmmmph!

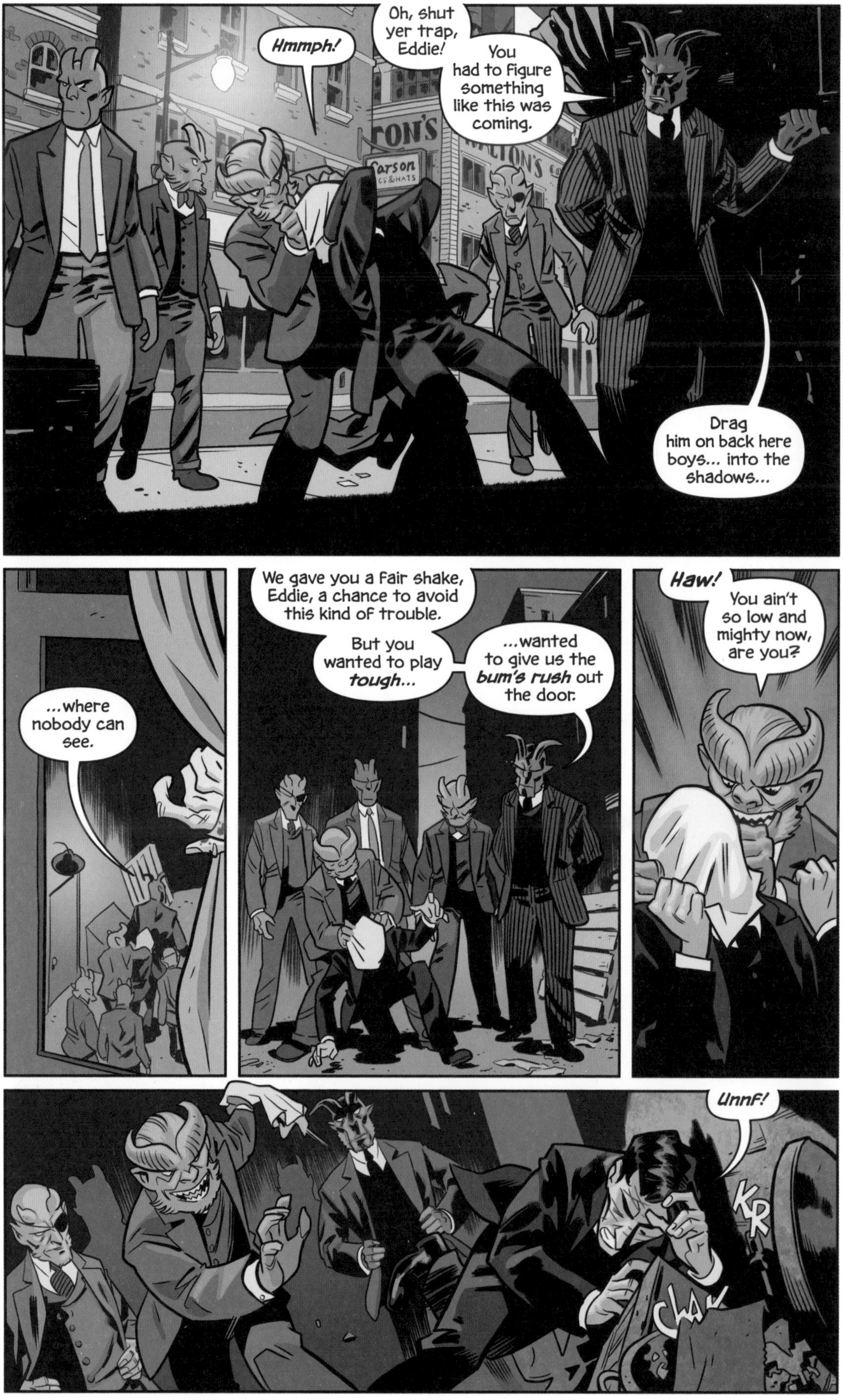
Hmmph!
Oh, shut yer trap, Eddie!
You had to figure something like this was coming.
TON'S
Carson
CS & HATS
Drag him on back here boys... into the shadows...
...where nobody can see.
We gave you a fair shake, Eddie, a chance to avoid this kind of trouble.
But you wanted to play *tough*...
...wanted to give us the *bum's rush* out the door.
Haw!
You ain't so low and mighty now, are you?
Unnf!
KR
CHAK

Maybe if you gents had told me why you were really at the club, I might've--

Oooof!

As I was asking, has Pauly Bones slithered his way back into yer life?

You know where he is?

Maybe he came to you--his old pal--asking fer help?

I might be inclined t-to answer your questions...

...but I j-just don't think you're asking *nicely* enough--

This nice enough for you?

KRAK

Hold off.

He can't talk if we beat his brains out his ears, now can he?

Besides, it's just not *civilized* to treat him so rough.

Glad you boys came to your senses.

Oh, we're gonna find Pauly with or without your help.

But we figured it was just about time to teach you a lesson.

See, Eddie. Yer just a *mortal*... and a cursed one at that...

...and you need to learn yer place!

SKLLLLSH!

You think because *Big Al* lets you run the Gehenna Room that yer *better* than us?

Hggk!

Everything you've got, we can take it away.

You ain't no demon, Eddie...

...so quit *pretending* to be one.

Watch out!

Don't let him touch you!

Sorry, Eddie. I don't think any of us are gonna give you a hand.

You want someone to take the cut for you...

...maybe you better find yerself a *human patsy!*

I think this is where I was when we started this little tale.

Me with my throat cut...

...bleeding out...

...feeling death pulling at me...

...dragging me down like I'm sinking in mud...

...and looking for someone...

...anyone...

...to act as a lifeline.

What the Hell.

It's not like I'm gonna get back into the Almighty's good graces any--

Hold your horses, Eddie.

No need to go and do something *heartless*, now is there?

T-Tony... ...didn't know you cared...

...about the poor and huddled masses...

What can I say? Big Al's got a *soft spot* for *gutter rats*.

He says if we don't look out for them, they might die off.

And if they die while they still got a soul, that's just pitching pennies down the drink.

And we come bearing gifts.

D-do I have to?

I mean... is it time?

I knew th-this moment was coming.

I just didn't expect...

...to be so scared.

Hell, I wake up every morning nearly pissing in my pants over what the day's gonna bring.

You don't hear *me* blubbering about it.

Don't forget what you *owe* Big Al.

S-Sorry about this.

But don't worry.

It'll be quick. It'll be any time...

Time's come to settle up.

Y-You really want to do me a favor?

Maybe you could give Bruno's flunkies a kick for me.

They were the ones who did the cutting.

Maybe later.

Right now, the boss wants to see you.

He wants to ask you a few questions about your pal Pauly Bones.

Seems like *everybody's* taking an interest in Pauly.

Exactly how much did he *lose?*

That's just it, Eddie.

"Guys like you, they always think they've got things figured out.

"But if you were half as wise as you think you are, you wouldn't keep landing yourself in these kind of situations.

"You think demons work the same way as you.

"Sure, they get caught up in all the same horsepucky that plagues mortals.

"That was bound to happen.

"You wallow in *filth* long enough, you start to *stink*.

"At the end of the day, though, they *ain't* human...

"...and they don't *want* the same things as you.

"You see... Pauly Bones didn't lose at all.

"He *won*...

"...and that makes him *dangerous*."

CHAPTER

2

A week ago.

I don't know what to say.

I don't want to *jinx* myself by saying I'm on a *hot streak*...

...but it sure *looks* like I'm on a hot streak.

And I figure you fellas know all about *hot*, right?

You...

...you wouldn't--

Get ya a refill, Mr. Risso?

Hnh?

I c'n serve myself.

Don't need you standin' over my shoulder with your smirks an' giggles.

Get lost.

CLINK

35

You know what, gentlemen... ...I think maybe I'll *drift*.

Way I see it, my *good fortune*--and my *welcome* in this fine establishment--can hold out for only so long.

Best to excuse myself--*graciously*--while I'm ahead.

You ain't goin' nowhere.

You wouldn't be *cheatin' us*, would you?

I'm *insulted*, Risso.

You all know me.

And if you know one thing about me, it's that Pauly Bones *doesn't* cheat.

An' who is it that always preachin' that tripe?

It was *you* who always says that.

You.

An' you just hope e'ryone else believes it.

Come on, Riz. Lay off.

Pauly's no cheat.

We gonna keep playing or not?

36

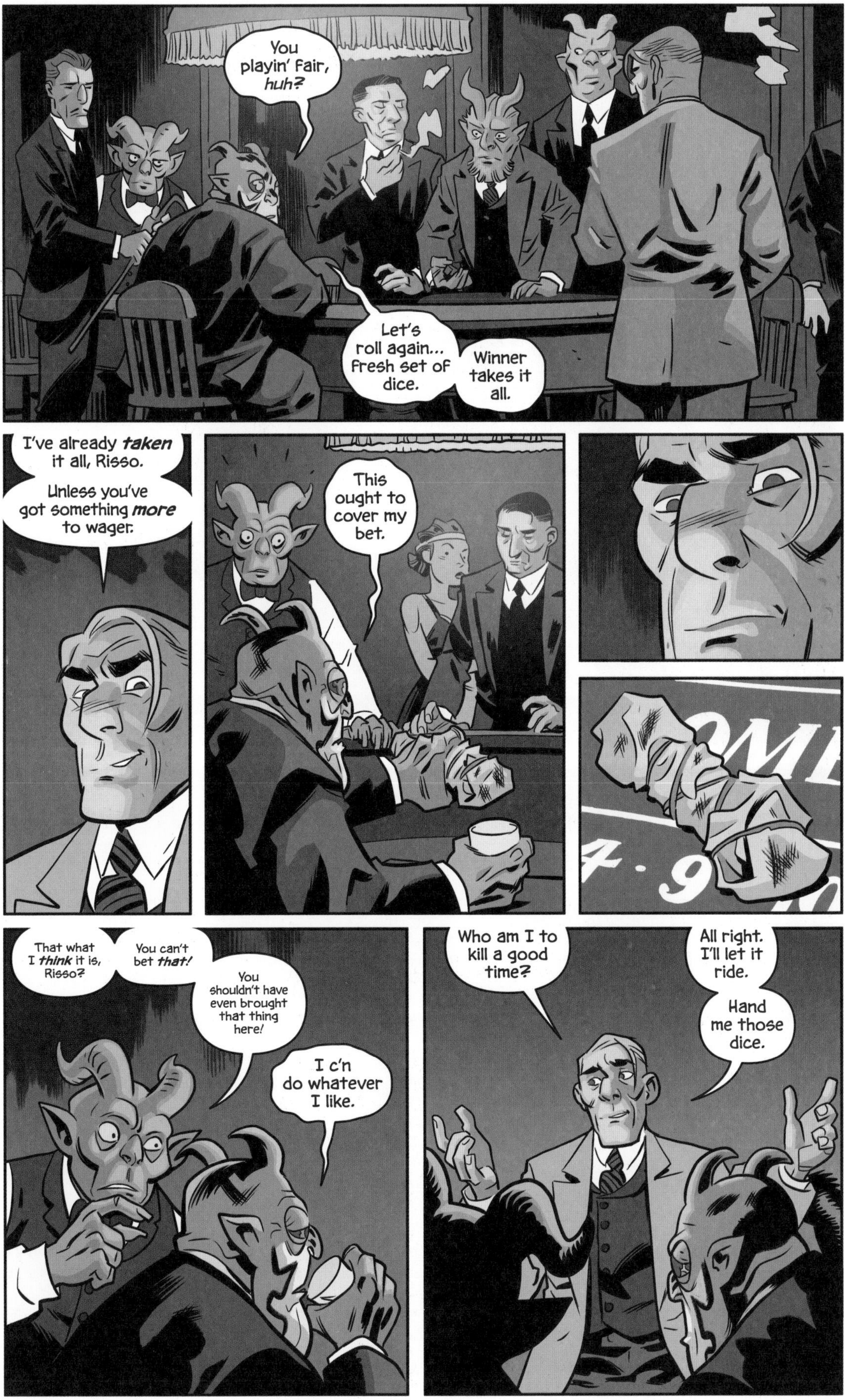
You playin' fair, *huh?*
Let's roll again... fresh set of dice.
Winner takes it all.
I've already *taken* it all, Risso.
Unless you've got something *more* to wager.
This ought to cover my bet.
That what I *think* it is, Risso?
You can't bet *that!*
You shouldn't have even brought that thing here!
I c'n do whatever I like.
Who am I to kill a good time?
All right. I'll let it ride.
Hand me those dice.

Now.

You know what your *problem* is, Eddie?

You mean besides the *obvious?*

I have a *few ideas,* yeah.

Yeah. Of course you do. Yeah.

You're a real *clever* guy.

You gonna tell me being "clever" is what gets me into trouble?

Nah, Eddie.

Did I say that to you before or something?

It *sounds* like something I might've said.

But I was just making *chatter* is all.

Being *smart's* better than being *stupid.*

Just like being *alive's* better than being *dead.*

We're here.

38

We're gonna walk from here.

That all right with you, Eddie?

I suppose.

My shoes might get a little muddy.

Give Eddie and me some room, boys.

But don't stray far.

You *catch up.*

Whatever you say, Tony.

Now...

...where was I?

Oh, yeah.

Your problem.

You got *plenty* of them, sure.

But this one, Eddie-- *this* is the one that's always biting you in the ass.

Everybody but you knows it.

Only you can't see it.

See, you think you can beat the *demons* at *their own game.*

You think that somewhere down the line you're gonna pull the double-cross of *all* double-crosses.

Never mind that you've only gotten yourself in more boiling water every time you've tried something of that nature.

When it comes to *deception* and *treachery* and *betrayal*--

--you're out of your depth.

Hey, Eddie.

Thanks for coming out all this way to see me.

I wasn't under the impression that I had a choice.

You got a smoke, Tony?

I'm fresh out.

Don't be like that, Tony. Don't be *petty*.

Give him a smoke.

Sure, Big Al.

Thanks.

What's the rumpus?

Why'd you drag me all the way out here?

You ever heard of the *Argent Clan?*

Yeah. I heard of them.

Heard more than I wanted.

Moonshiners out of Nag's Hollow.

Their corn mash is supposed to be good...

...but not worth the trouble.

Supposed to be taking a meeting with their *patriarch*...

...but he's running late.

This burning candles at both ends business is running me ragged, Eddie.

That's a shame.

If it's all the same, though, I'd like to be far from here when they show up.

Tell me what you want and I'll be on my merry way.

I've known you a long time, Eddie.

Not sure I've ever seen you *scared* before.

Not scared now.

But I'm a busy man, just like you.

If we could cut to--

Hold that thought.

My other appointment's here.

Big Al was wrong about me being frightened.

But he wasn't *that* far off, either.

The Argent Clan made me *uncomfortable*.

Years of inbreeding and rough living and hard times had turned them into something *less* than human.

They were cunning and cruel and dangerous.

The swamps they called home were full of *dead bodies* and *buried secrets*.

But that's not why they made me *uneasy*.

What I found most unsettling about them wasn't what they had done.

It was what they *hadn't* done, not in all their dealings with demons.

If rumors were to be believed...

...not a single member of the Argent Family had ever even considered offering up their *soul* in trade.

That just didn't sit right with me.

It troubled me, though... worried at me... that a bunch of inbred bumpkins could manage to hold onto their immortal Family jewels...

...when I could not.

I gotta wonder, though... the Argents are no saints... no angels...

You bring something for me to sample?

...but they ain't *damned*, either, at least not the same as me.

When they look at Big Al, what do they see?

A *demon* or a *man?*

43

Does he recognize Al's true nature?

Yes.

Yes, I believe this will do just fine.

Want a *taste*, Eddie?

I'll pass.

I got plenty of coffin varnish waiting for me at the club.

Does *anyone?*

We can deliver as usual, by the boxcar full.

You understand, of course, that the *price* is going *up.*

How's that now?

You sent your boys out to the Hollow.

Thought to *strong-arm* us.

And don't bother pointing your finger at anyone else. We know it was you.

Business. Simple business.

You can't blame a businessman for trying to *widen* his *margins...*

...any more than I can blame you for the fact that my "boys" *never* made it back home.

Musta got *lost.*

Just the same...

...you either pay up, or maybe *Bruno Roarke* or one of them *other competitors* will.

Nah.

The Argents didn't see Al's true colors *at all.*

44

KRK

BRAKKA--BRAKKA--BRAKKA

KRAK

BLAM

BOOM!

KKA--BRAKK

POW!

KKA--B

BLAM!

BRAKKA--B

POW!

KRAK

BLAM!

N-nuuh--

CRK

What are you reaching for, tough guy?

If you wanted to make it out of this scuffle...

...the *last* thing you should have been doing was reaching for a gun.

BLAM

Sons...

...sons of bitches...

...killed us...

...killed us every one...

Not *all* of you.

You're still breathing.

Have a drink.

And think about all your friends and family... back at Nag's Hollow... who are still alive, too...

...for now, at least.

W-What...

...what do you want?

You want the mash... it's yours.

You think I don't know that already?

It's gonna take a lot more than booze to get you out of this one, Mr. Argent.

Then... then what?

All right...

...yes...

...all right...

Going somewhere, Eddie?

The boss hasn't had a chance to talk to you just yet.

He didn't bring me out here to talk to me.

He showed me what he wanted to show me.

It's like I said, Eddie.

You're sharp as a tack.

Big Al wants to remind you just how much a *soul's* really worth. You catch on right quick.

Yeah, but what's any of that got to do with me?

What's it got to do with *Pauly Bones* and whatever the Hell he won?

You got yourself a real *fakeroo artist* holed up in your club, Eddie.

He'll sell you a *bridge* if you let him.

You can't protect him forever.

Do yourself a favor and hand Pauly over to Big Al.

I'll think on it, Tony.

Tell Al.

I'll have plenty of time while I'm ankling it back to town.

Plenty of time to consider my options.

What?

No apple for teacher?

This don't say much about you, Eddie...

...or maybe it says *everything* worth knowing.

Can't even use the front door at your own club...

...moving in the shadows...

...like *us.*

No sense in tracking mud... and blood... across the carpets.

Better to use the back entrance.

What can I do for you, *Goldy?*

Heard you paid *Deidra* a visit.

Heard you were catching up on *old times.*

Word travels fast, I suppose.

Don't tell me, you're all sore I didn't stop by to say hello while I was in the old neighborhood.

Deidra says you were asking about *Pauly Bones.*

Says she don't think you'd come around asking without a reason.

Says Pauly might be back in town.

50

Yeah? What else did she say?

I know it had to be something to get the lot of you crawling out into the public eye.

She says Pauly's come back into town to make good on a *promise*.

What *sort* of promise?

I bet you can just *imagine*...

...that you can just *dream*...

...because you're *one* of us.

If he can make good with Deidra...

...maybe he's got the *horns* to make good for the *rest* of us.

We can get out, Eddie. All of us.

We can get out *clean*.

Don't believe everything you hear about Pauly.

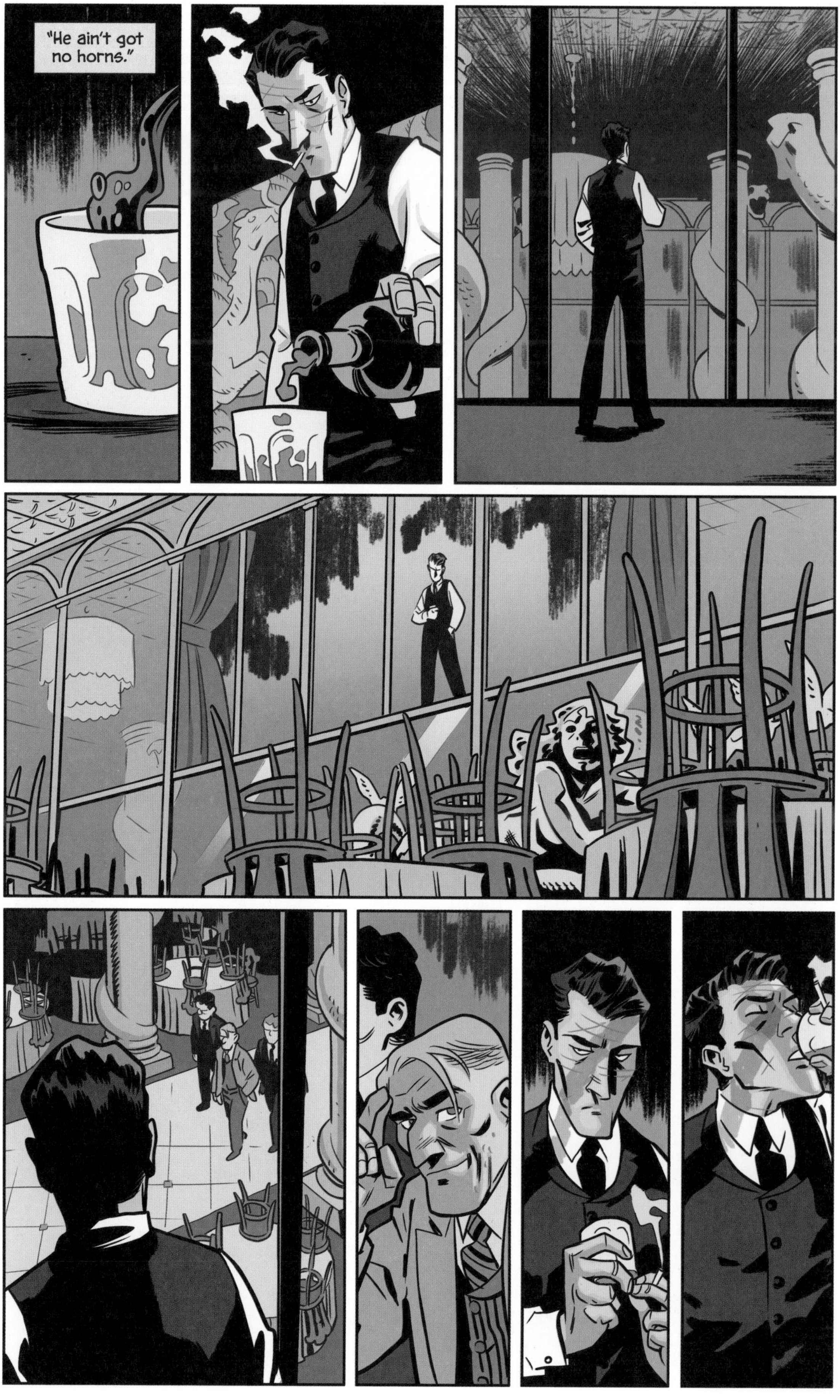
"He ain't got no horns."

Eduardo, Eduardo, Eduardo.

This place you've got here, it's **something else**.

You've come a **long way**.

Back when we were running around with **Sophie** and the **Wyrm**...

...you ever think you'd end up here?

Whatever happened to her anyhow?

I already asked you about Soph, didn't I?

And you didn't want to talk about it.

I get it. **Sore subject**.

Well, what about that **brother** of yours? How's--

What did you win?

Hey, Eduardo.

I don't know if I ever--

What is it?

53

It's a **key**, all right?

At least, I **think** it's a key.

Let's see it.

I **know** you didn't leave it **unattended** in your room.

You've got it in your **pocket**, right?

I was planning on showing you, Eddie.

I mean, I came here so I could bring you in on this.

You came here because you know demons have **rules** that even they have to follow.

You know they swore that the Gehenna Room is **off limits**.

You felt **safe** here.

Well, yeah.

That, too.

All right.

If it's a key, what does it **unlock?**

No idea.

But the demons **want** it, right? It must be **important** to them.

Important enough... that we might be able to make a **trade**.

A trade.

You know what I'm after.

"And I can cut you in."

Whu--

What is this?

This... this ain't right.

What do you want?

This isn't about what I want, Risso.

If it was about what I want, I'd be far, far from this place...

...this *den of iniquity.*

My *employer,* though...

...and *your* employer, for that matter...

...wants me here.

He wants me to *punish* you for what you did...

...for your *bad bet.*

I... I always settle up.

I never make a bet I can't cover.

Well, I know you do.

And there's the rub.

That's why I was sent here.

That's why I had to partake in all this... *unpleasantness.*

I can tell you where the *reliquary* went, all right?

I'll tell you and you can just let me go.

You'll never see me again.

It's... *Pauly Bones* you want.

He skipped town with it.

I know, Risso. I know.

Everybody knows.

Everybody knows that a lowlife like Pauly Bones now holds something mortal man wasn't ever even supposed to *see.*

All because of a roll of the dice.

So... before I go settle matters with Mr. Bones... why don't we see how the *dice* serve you today, hmm?

Let's see if *Lady Luck* wants you to have another chance.

BLAM!

CHAPTER

3

SLAP!

All right, all right.

I had that one coming.

You still got it, Deidra.

How *long* has it been?

How long without a *word?*

I figure you were keeping tabs on me.

You know *why* I left.

I told you I wasn't coming back unless I could deliver on my *promises.*

I never held you to your word.

That would have been a *waste.*

Well then, this time the joke's on *you*.

Because this time--*this time*-- ol' Pauly Bones came through.

You...

How?

I don't feel any different--

I got the demons by the *horns*, doll.

It's just a matter of time.

What Pauly's saying is he's got a line on the prize.

But he hasn't fished it in just yet.

There are still bargains to be struck... and they might blow up in our faces before we're through.

Jeeze, Eddie.

Would it kill you to think *positive* just this once?

It sure as Hell won't keep me alive.

A bargain?

With the *demons?*

You said you'd made good on your promises... on all your sweet whispers...

...but you've got *nothing.*

There's no *Chinese angle* to this, Deidra. We've got something the demons *want*.

They'll *trade*.

Or they'll *kill* you.

Or maybe they'll make things *worse*.

Don't worry. I've got *Eddie* to watch my back.

This is gonna *work out*.

Just *go*.

Just hang tight a little longer.

I'm *close* now. I *know* it.

I wouldn't have come back if I wasn't *sure*.

Just a little longer.

What's with this guy?

After the beating we gave Eddie, I'd think he'd stay away from this place.

But he just keeps coming back.

Maybe he's *sweet* on the dame.

That ain't it.

He's making a play.

Him and his pal, they've come into a spot of good fortune.

Got themselves a pretty little trinket.

There they are.

Let's just grab them right now and shake 'em down.

Then we can go get a *steak*.

Do yourself a favor and stop *thinking*.

It only gets in the way of your *real* talents.

They ain't gonna have it on them. They'll have hidden it by now.

We'll follow them.

Spotted the car as soon as I stepped onto the street.

Bruno Roarke's **trouble boys.**

Demons have gotten so accustomed to hiding in plain sight...

You see 'em, too?

...they barely put any *effort* into tailing someone.

What should we do?

Get in the car.

Go about our business.

They'll be right behind us...

...watching our every move.

Let 'em.

I've got a feeling they'll back off once they see where we're headed.

I know I should keep my *opinions* to myself...

...but when I've got an *itch*, I scratch...

...sometimes til the skin is raw and bleeding.

She doesn't really give a damn about you.

You realize that, right?

Hnh?

What are you yapping about?

Deidra.

All this time, she wasn't pining over you.

She was pining over what you *might* do for her.

Same old Eddie.

You think you've got *everybody* figured out, don't you?

Let it drift, then.

Forget I said anything.

We ain't cut from the same cloth, Eddie.

That's why you can't see what I'm trying to do.

I'm not in this for myself.

Maybe you can't understand that.

Yeah, Pauly.

You're a right gee.

I'm the asshole.

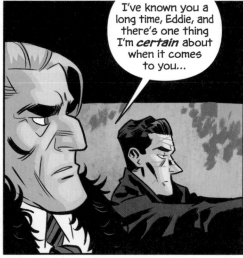

I've known you a long time, Eddie, and there's one thing I'm *certain* about when it comes to you...

...one thing that-- believe it or not--sets you and me apart.

You ain't never made a promise you didn't break.

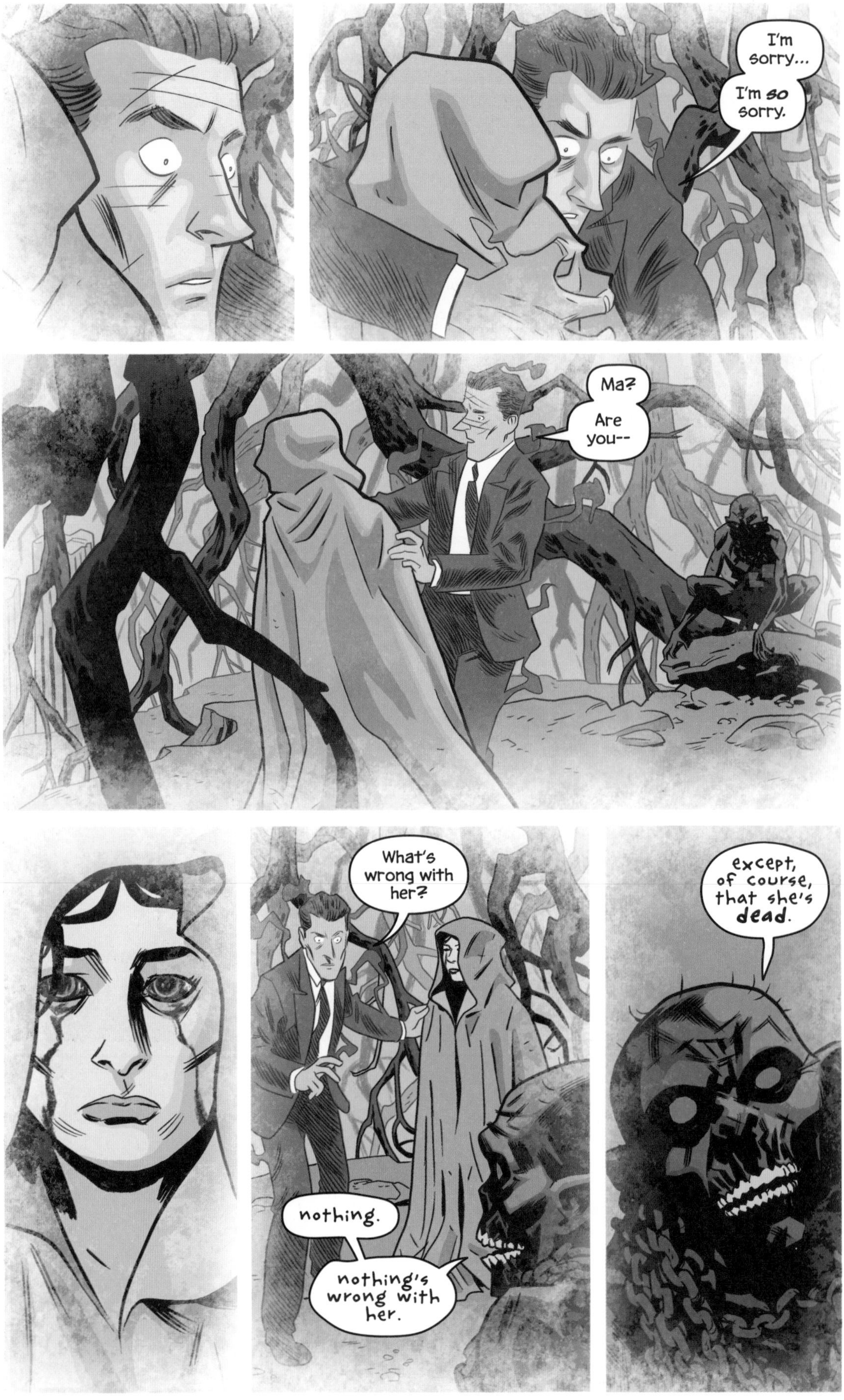
I'm sorry...
I'm **so** sorry.
Ma?
Are you--
What's wrong with her?
nothing.
nothing's wrong with her.
except, of course, that she's **dead**.

BUT you *knew* that.

you knew that before you came here.

you knew...

...because you *killed* her.

What do you know about it?

all these little boxes.

all of them tell stories.

your mother's story is here... *somewhere*.

I want to talk to her.

You can't.

she's *lost*.

it is her *curse* to *wander* this realm, just as it is yours to wander another.

Fuck curses.

I'll find a way, Ma.

I'll *free* you... *somehow*.

I... *promise*.

That's what I thought.

We'll wait here.

This is *close* enough.

We'll *lose* them.

I say we stay on them.

I ain't *afraid* of those woods.

You want to follow them, go on, hoof it.

But this ain't about being *afraid*.

There are *treaties* to be honored.

You ain't got any use for the *old ways*.

Suit yourself.

But them that live in those woods, they still respect *ancient traditions*.

And you don't want to blaspheme in their territory.

We're losing daylight.

Always do in this place.

Eyes to the front.

It makes it easier.

You don't want to stare into those woods for too long.

This the *first time* you set foot on *Verlochin* land?

That's right.

I'm not an *idiot*.

Heh.

I've been here a *bunch* of times.

You sure you want to do the talking?

This is *my* deal.

I can handle a few *demons*.

There's demons and then there's *demons*.

What's the distinction?

TAP TAP

You're about to find out.

CREEEEEAAAK

Which of us talked the other into this, anyway?

If it's just the same, I'm gonna blame you.

You said it yourself, Pauly.

Your deal.

For a second there, it felt like the **good old days.**

Like it was with the **old gang,** before everything went to shit.

I remind myself that those times are **long gone.**

And they weren't that good, either.

We're not **kids** anymore.

The old crew is gone, and we're not even **friends,** Pauly and me.

It's **safer** that way.

...*persecution,* children, is not the province of *mortal souls.*

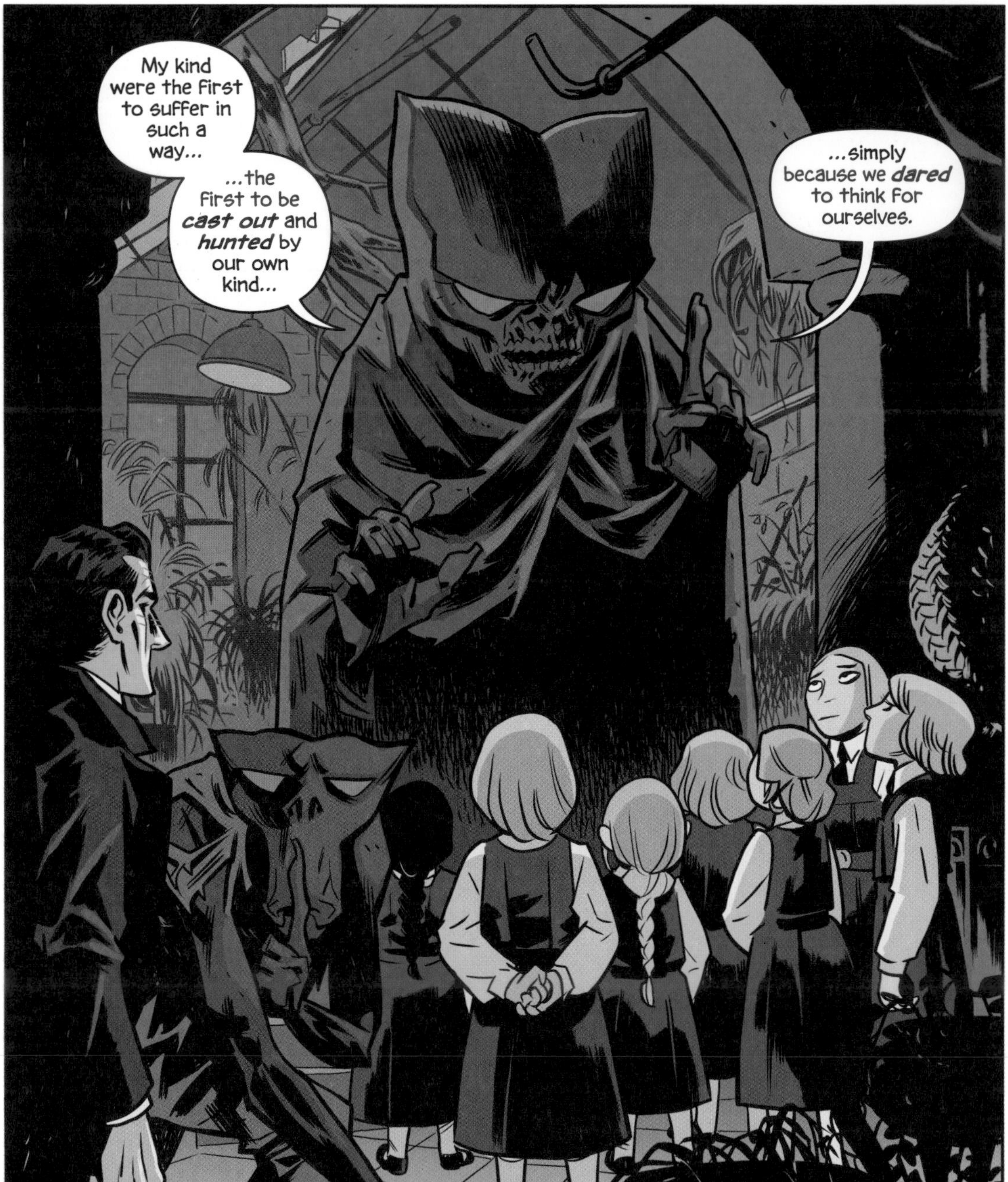
My kind were the first to suffer in such a way...
...the first to be **cast out** and **hunted** by our own kind...
...simply because we **dared** to think for ourselves.

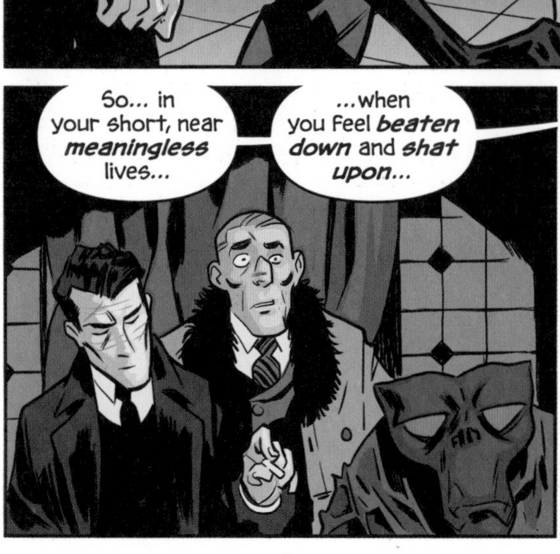
So... in your short, near **meaningless** lives...
...when you feel **beaten down** and **shat upon**...

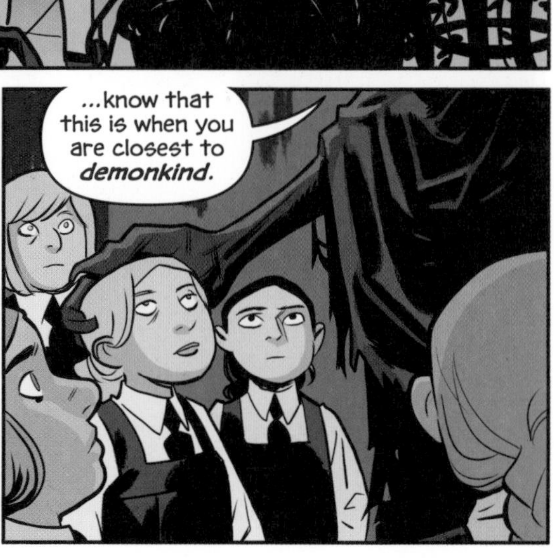
...know that this is when you are closest to **demonkind**.

That's enough for today, children.

Go... and remember your *lessons*...

...for soon you'll be sent out into the world...

...to do our bidding.

This is becoming a *habit*, Eddie.

If I didn't know better, I'd think that you *liked* visiting us.

Oh, I love it.

The smell of rot and mildew and your *bullshit* is good for the soul.

What have you brought us today?

Yes.

What have you brought us?

Yes! Yes!

What have you brought?

Brought!

Yes!

What have you brought?

Like you said.

This is *your* deal.

Make your case.

I think you gentlemen *know* why I'm here. You might live out in the sticks, but I'm guessing word travels fast.

And you probably realize I have *plenty* of potential buyers for what I'm selling.

So I feel like I'm in a position to cut right to the chase.

We want *souls.*

They been in there a while.

Bet it feels longer for them than it does for us.

Maybe they already struck a bargain.

Maybe. But I sez they didn't bring the *key* with them. They hid it somewhere before ever approaching the Verlochin.

If they make a deal, they'll have to go dig up the key.

And that's when we take it.

But if they already reached an agreement...

...if they have accepted the Verlochin's terms...

...the *covenants* say we can't--

I didn't *witness* the transaction, did you?

And I ain't gonna ask Eddie and his friends for details when we steal the key.

You mugs need to learn how to work the system a little--

Hey! Somebody's coming!

Who's out there? Speak up before we--

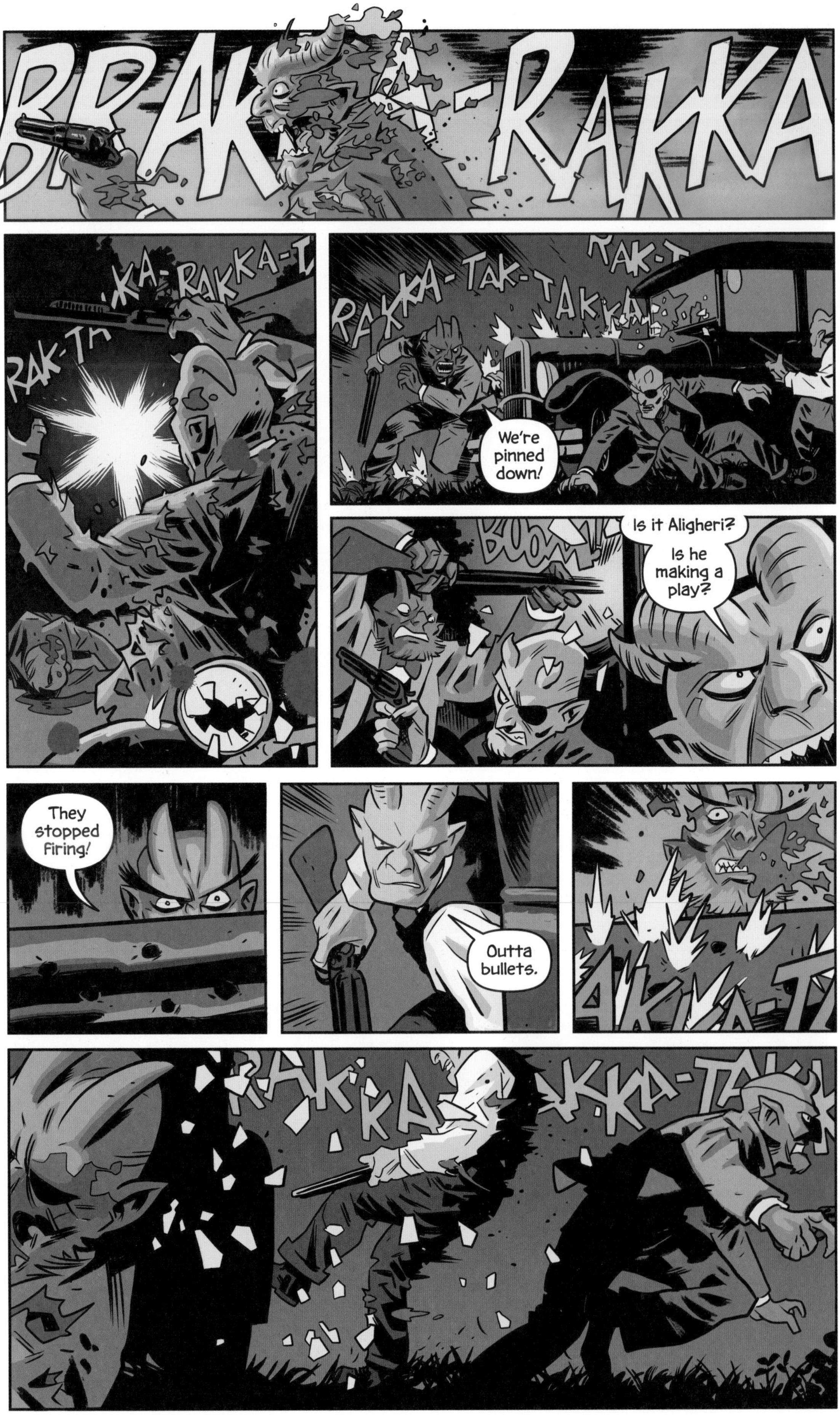
-RAKKA
RAK-TA
KA-RAKKA-T
RAKKA-TAK-TAKKA
We're pinned down!
Is it Aligheri?
Is he making a play?
They stopped firing!
Outta bullets.

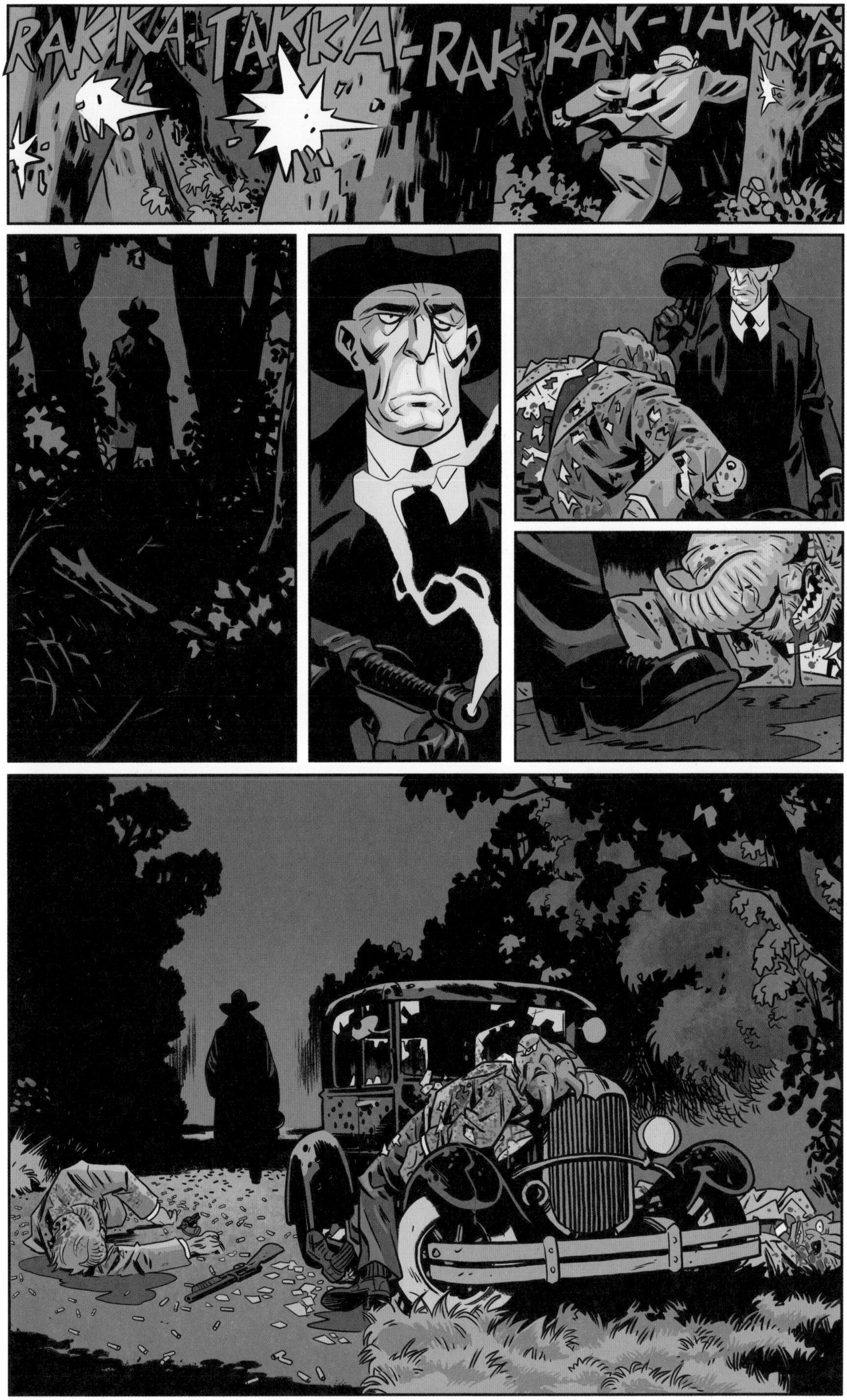
RAKKA-TAKKA-RAK-RAK-RAK-TAKKA

"You're asking too much..."

...more than you should, actually...

...especially since you know *nothing* about the key.

I know *enough.*

I know you *want* it.

But you're asking for the return of *mortal souls...*

...souls we took in fair trade.

And this will be a fair trade, too.

Come on, fellas.

A couple of souls can't possibly mean that much to you.

And I suppose *you* want your soul back as well.

For *starters.*

78

You'll understand if we need time to *discuss* your terms.

Yeah, sure.

Do what you've got to do.

But don't take too long, yeah?

Like I said, there are *other* interested parties.

But no other that can give you what it is you desire.

So don't try to strong-arm us.

We'll take as long as we want, and you'll *bide* that time.

If I--

C'mon, Pauly.

You're not going to get more of an answer than that, not right now.

Let's go.

Don't worry...

...we'll be *in touch*.

They're watching as we leave.

I could look back at the house, but I'd never spot them. So I don't bother.

They're better at hiding than Roarke's men.

But the Verlochin are there.

I can *feel* them.

Just like I can feel that we're about to get the needle.

There's no way the demons give us what we want...

...not free and clear...

...and not the *both* of us.

We'd be *fools* to think otherwise.

We're not getting out of this *unscathed*.

You play with blades, *somebody's* gonna get *cut*.

Sometimes, *everybody* bleeds.

CHAPTER

4

None of us were there when Deidra parted ways with her mortal soul.

We didn't see how it went down.

It's different for every poor sap who scrawls their bloody name on a contract.

But I can guess how it played out.

Hello, Vic.

Uh... hey... Deidra.

How're you doing?

I wondered if I'd find you here.

When we made our date for tonight, I didn't realize we were supposed to meet at the club.

Did we have plans tonight? Musta slipped my mind.

Hey, Dee, I want you to meet my new friend here.

Uh...

Sally.

That's right. This is Sally.

We go way back, me and her.

Hmph!

Aw, come on, Dee! Don't be like that!

Tragic. Simply tragic.

84

A beautiful woman like yourself...

...treated like a *cancelled stamp* by all these buffoons...

...and all because of what?

Because you're a few years older than these little minxes who are flouncing around?

I'm not *that* much older than they are.

Of course not.

But what a difference just a few years can make, *hmm?*

And--really--what *fools* these *mortals* be.

You're one of *them,* aren't you?

My dear...

...I'm your *best friend.*

Yes, you have. And there's no judgement, not from me.

There's no blame...

Don't get ahead of yourself.

I'm not sure I want to do this.

I still haven't made up my mind.

...not from any of us.

I don't know. This...

...It doesn't feel right.

I find these matters are best dealt with quickly.

Like tearing off a scab.

Oh--!

All you need to do is sign.

And then all your worries will be as temporary and transient as *youth itself.*

Ah--

Oh...

Oh, no.

What is--?

It is *done*.

And now you see us without the *blindfold* of a *soul*.

You have received our *blessing*.

I thought... I would be *young* again.

I thought I would be *beautiful*.

You wanted to be *desirable*.

And so you are.

Desirability has nothing to do with *youth*. With *beauty*.

Are *we* beautiful? No... and you still sought us out.

We have given you what you wanted.

And now... you are our creature.

No matter how it happened, the end result was the same.

Another name in the ledger...

...another mortal screwed over by demon kind.

KRA

SCRMBL-CRNCH

SKREEEEEE

N-nice driving, Eddie.

You're alive, ain't ya?

M-maybe not for long, though.

That must've been Bruno Roarke's boys.

Damn! They've got horns!

Didn't expect them to come after us like that, not so close to--

No.

Whoever hit us...

...they whacked Bruno's guys, too.

Who're we dealing with--?

BRAKKA-RAKKA-RAK

BRAKK

BR

BRAK

You wanna know who wants us dead?

Why don't you go ask him?

Tell ya what.

Let me hold that heater and *you* do the talking!

BRAKKA-RAK RAKKA

We're sitting ducks here!

We gotta get some cover... put some distance between that Tommy and our asses!

When I start shooting back, you run for it!

KAKKA-BRAK

BLAM BLAM BLA

Pauly Bones doesn't look back.

Can't say that I blame him.

RAKKA—

I'm not one to play *hero*, myself.

All things considered, I was halfway hoping the goon with the gat would chase Pauly and give me a chance to make myself scarce.

Caught a glimpse of the guy when I took my shot.

Human from the looks of him, *not* a demon.

Not sure if that makes me *less* or *more* afraid of him.

Playing with demons for too long can turn you into a real *monster*.

BRAKKA-RAK

I should know.

Mortals are a nasty bunch on their own.

When they want something bad enough...

...they can be more dangerous than any demon that's ever crawled up outta Hell.

Deidra! Have a drink with me!

Would you do me the honor of a dance?

Wanna go somewhere a little more romantic?

Oh, boys! You certainly do know how to flatter a girl!

But I'm afraid you must excuse me for just a moment while I powder my nose.

Good evening, Deidra!

You're not running off are you?

Don't leave before we have a drink together!

Hey there, Deidra. Fancy meeting you here.

Pauly--

I told you not to come here.

Yeah, I know.

But I wanted to see for myself why you wanted me to stay away.

And, look at you, a choice bit of calico here among the jackals.

You're a sweet boy. You really are.

But you're not very smart.

I guess not.

I fell for you, didn't I?

On that count, neither one of us is all that bright.

Sorry, Pauly. Not here, not now.

The bank's closed.

Let's blow this popsicle stand, Deidra. We'll get out of here, go somewhere quiet.

Just the two of us.

I can't, Pauly. I want to, but I can't. Not tonight.

Just go home, all right?

Go home and I'll come around tomorrow.

Please.

Shit!

LADIES

Hello, Deidra. Tell me about your friend.

Who? The wet blanket in the hall?

Oh, he's nobody important.

Is that so?

That's right.

But I've found several good candidates here tonight.

They're falling all over themselves to get to me.

It won't take long to convince them to make their mark on one of those contracts of yours.

That's nice. I think, though, I've seen what I want. I like the looks of that gentleman caller of yours.

What was his name?

Pauly.

Yes. Pauly.

That's the one.

That's the *soul* I want you to bring me tonight.

The demons will treat you plenty poorly if they're given half the chance... but they have rules.

It's free will...

...that little thing demons covet so fiercely...

...that really makes us mortals *nasty*.

≥hff≤

≥hnf≤

Pauly, Pauly, Pauly.

You've found yourself in a spot of trouble, haven't you?

Yes, trouble tends to find you, doesn't it?

Especially when you throw in with your old friend Eddie.

Is that one of your boys?

You sent someone after us?

You're trying to have me and Eddie killed?

Nonsense.

That's not how the Verlochin work, Pauly.

You should know better.

All right. If you didn't send him, who did?

I do not know who sent him.

But I know who he is.

"He is called, in some circles, *the Exorcist.*

"He *loathes* demons... has no compunction against *killing* them on sight... but he *works* for demons, too."

Why would he do that?

If he hates your kind so much, why throw in with them?

Because my infernal brethren have something to *offer* him.

Everyone has something they want.

And it's a simple trade, *ideals* for *desires.*

Take you, for example, Pauly.

You must know the Verlochin will never return three souls.

But we might be persuaded to return two.

We know you and Eddie are *friends.*

But what you should ask yourself is this...

...just how *close* is that friendship?

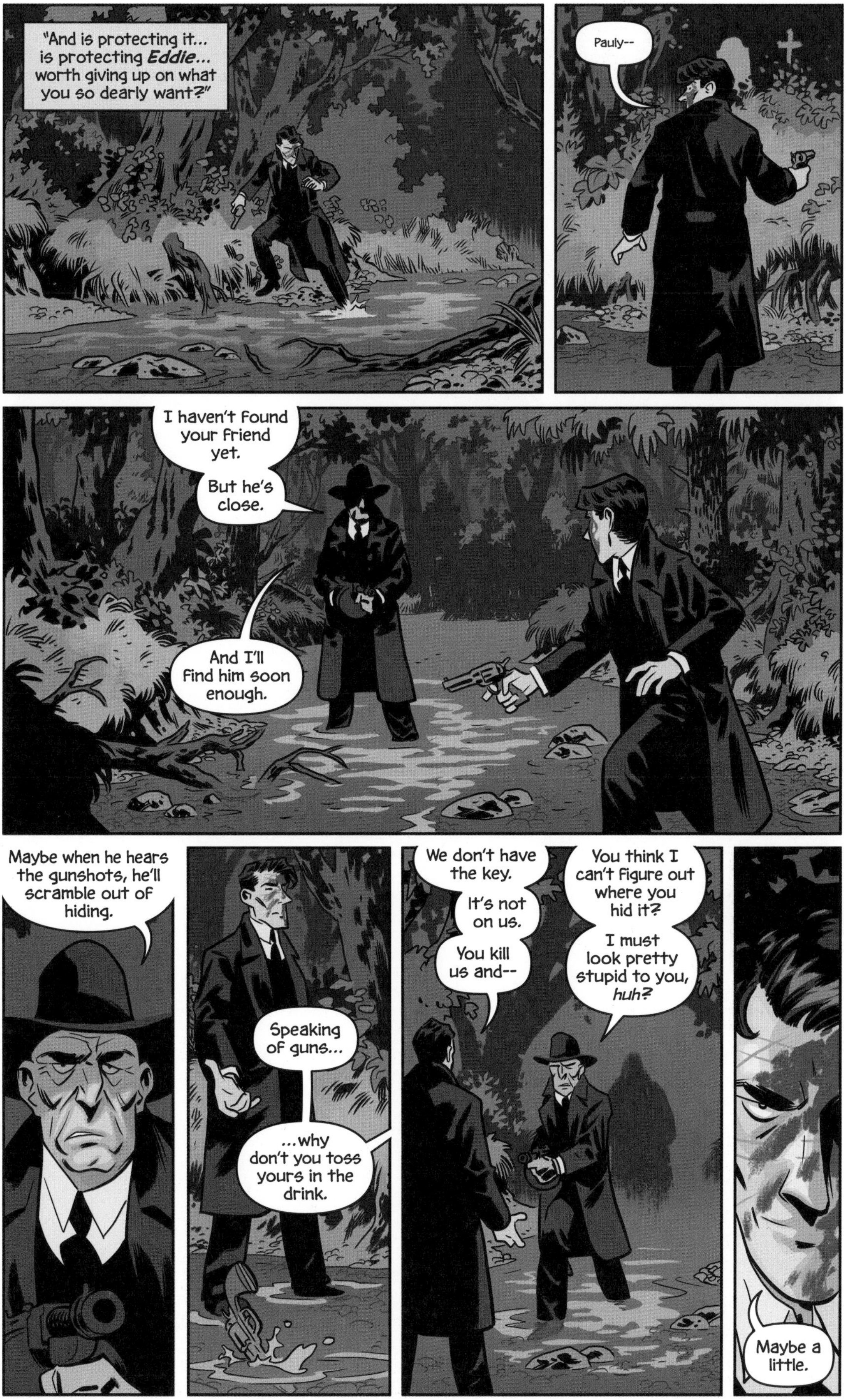
"And is protecting it... is protecting *Eddie*... worth giving up on what you so dearly want?"
Pauly--
I haven't found your friend yet.
But he's close.
And I'll find him soon enough.
Maybe when he hears the gunshots, he'll scramble out of hiding.
Speaking of guns...
...why don't you toss yours in the drink.
We don't have the key.
It's not on us.
You kill us and--
You think I can't figure out where you hid it?
I must look pretty stupid to you, *huh?*
Maybe a little.

CHOK!

SPLOOSH!

Took you long enough, Pauly.

What can I say?

I needed to catch my second wind.

You think he's dead?

He's not looking too good.

I think you cracked his skull.

Serves him right.

Not like he was going to do us any favors.

Hey, Eddie.

Let's just go, huh?

I don't think I want to stay out here much longer.

Pauly's voice is shaking. It's a tone I've heard before with other people.

He's come to a crossroads. He's made a choice-- one he's none-too-sure about.

There's bad things out here in the woods.

Only thing I can't tell is whether he took whatever deal he was offered...

...or if he *refused.*

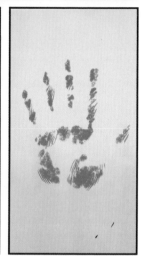

Deidra! There you are!

Come over here, dear! Join me at my table!

It feels like you've been gone forever!

Don't touch me!

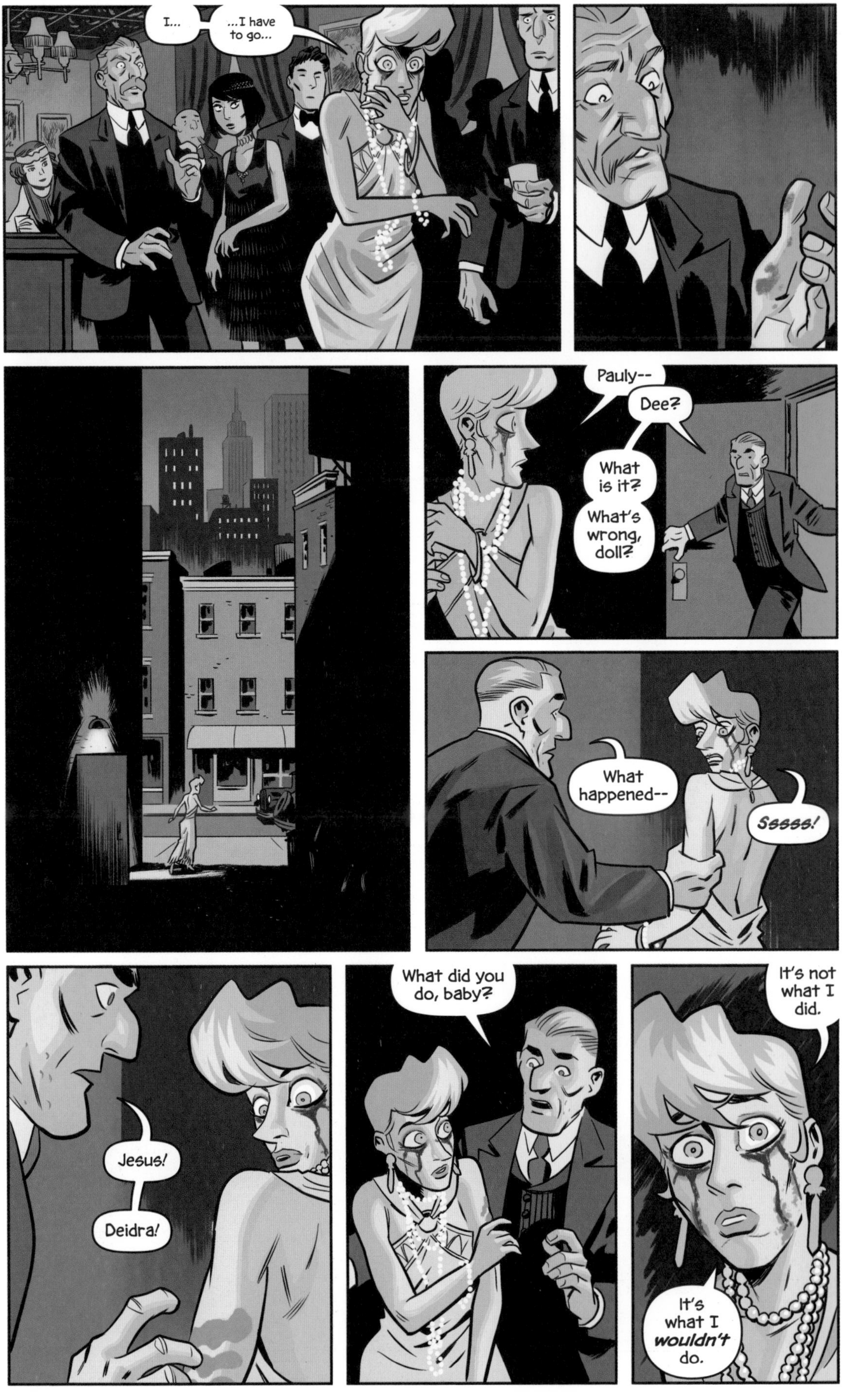

I...
...I have to go...
Pauly--
Dee?
What is it?
What's wrong, doll?
What happened--
Sssss!
Jesus!
Deidra!
What did you do, baby?
It's not what I did.
It's what I *wouldn't* do.

Even in a city overrun with demons...

...there are only a few places where you won't find one of the infernal.

You want to hide something from one of the families...

...you take it to a place they dare not tread.

Like I said, though, demons don't run the table when it comes to double-dealing.

Not even close.

Pauly Bones! Welcome, welcome!

What brings you out on such a dismal day?

Demons might've been born into treachery.

I need to make a withdrawal.

Of course! Of course!

Follow me!

But people only get there through *practice*--and a lot of it.

It must be important, coming out in the rain like you did.

Yes?

It's all right. Don't worry about it.

You don't have to tell me.

I was just making small talk before we get down to business.

There you are.

Just lock up when you're finished.

Bring the key back to me up front.

It's all important.

Otherwise you wouldn't bring it here, would you?

And me...

...I've put in more practice hours than most.

I should've figured it.

You waited until Pauly and me were separated.

Is this when you try to convince us both to stab the other in the back?

I'm sure you can appreciate an attention to all the angles, Eddie.

You're wasting your time, pal.

This was Pauly's deal.

I might not tell him this, but I think he's onto something.

Seems to me, a good many demons want what--

Silence!

I have little patience for debate.

You will hear my offer and that will be the end of our discussion.

We will not return your soul, Eddie.

That is not our way.

But we can still bargain with you.

But bring the key to us... bring it straight away...

...and we'll give you something you want.

We'll tell you... how you can communicate with your dead mother once more.

Double-dealing, that comes easy.

Avoiding the temptation of another devil's pact, not so much.

Goddammit, Eddie!

CRAK!

I feel bad, crossing Pauly this way.

After all, he was only trying to keep a promise.

This key was his ticket.

I've made promises, too.

But I never made a one of them to Pauly Bones.

So I guess I can skip the guilt and get on with what I've got to do.

CHAPTER

5

There are better places to drink, sure.

Back at the *Gehenna Room*, I could drink for free.

the. **BLACK RAT** TAVERN

But it ain't the same.

This place... this bar... has **history**...

The kind that sticks to the bottom of your shoes...

...the kind that crawls over you when you're passed out in the gutter.

History.

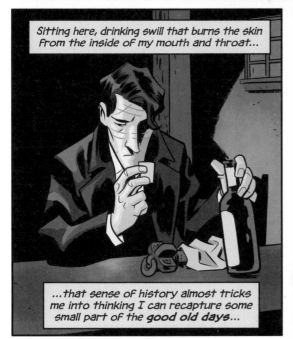

Sitting here, drinking swill that burns the skin from the inside of my mouth and throat...

...that sense of history almost tricks me into thinking I can recapture some small part of the **good old days**...

...from back before I was such a **bastard**.

Heh.

"When the Hell was that?"

Now I take a lot of duff from you, Eddie...

...but I don't think I can let you talk about Deidra in that tone.

Didn't realize I was *using* a tone, Pauly...

...not unless *honesty* just sounds *different* rolling off the tongue.

I'm not gonna hear this from you.

You don't know what you're talking about.

You don't know her.

I know her *type*.

Yeah?

And what "type" is that?

Choose your next words real carefully.

Pauly! Eddie!

What are you *arguing* for, *huh?*

You two are *pals*, yeah?

And you're *good boys*.

Here, here.

Both of you have an apple, *huh?*

Chew on them while you think about how you talk to one another, yeah?

Be good boys, *huh?*

Good boys don't argue with their pals.

She's a *fetch*, Pauly.

She sniffs out prey for the horn-heads.

She damns people on their behalf.

Sooner or later...

...*everybody* plays that game.

You should have a care, though, Eddie.

You got a real knack for burning bridges, but I'm not sure you can afford to torch another one.

Way I see it...

...I'm just about the only friend you've got left.

Mind if I go out the back?

Suit yourself.

Ain't this something, Eddie?

Seems like every time we run into you, you're sneaking out the back door of some bar.

Goldy and the others... they're *cursed*, too.

That means they sold their souls, then were stupid enough to try and swindle the demons in some way.

Just like Deidra.

Just like me, too, I suppose.

And you always seem to know where to look, Goldy.

I'm beginning to wonder if you've been tailing me.

Only they want their curses lifted... their souls back.

Again... just like Deidra.

Hand it over, why don't you?

I wouldn't want this to turn ugly.

And that puts us at *cross purposes*.

Pauly and Deidra sent you after me, didn't they?

I can tell that key is weighing heavy on your shoulders, Eddie.

Otherwise, you would've went to the Verlochin instead of coming here to drown your guilt.

Just give us what we want and you can breathe easy.

Sorry.

I don't know what you're talking about.

And I have places to--

You're not going anywhere...

...not til we get what we came for.

FFWUMP!

CRAK!

KROOMPF!

Well, *Fuck* me...

WHUMP

Ooof!

THWOK!

I wish it didn't have to be this way, Eddie.

But we're trying to get our souls back.

There's no time for *civility*.

Search him.

This it?

Y-you're damn fools...

...Deidra and Pauly...

...they don't care about you...

...they don't give *two shits* about *your* curses...

And *you* do?

Sorry, Eddie.

Deidra's been right there with us all this time.

And you left us for something better.

"Just wait right here, Eddie, all right?"

113

...feel her out, y'know?

"Just give me a minute to talk to her..."

If you don't need me here, I can find somewhere--

Stay, Eddie. I want you to.

You know how this is gonna work out.

At least... you can guess.

And I figure I'll need my pal here with me.

If you know how it's gonna shake out... why tell her at all?

It's just something I need to do.

You know?

Hell, no, I don't.

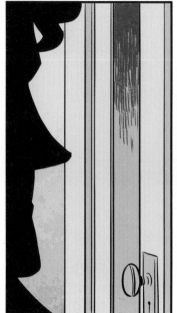

114

...what did you think I would say, Pauly?

Did you think I'd be *grateful?*

Did you think I'd throw my arms around you and thank the Lord for what you've done?

N-no, Deidra. No.

I figured you'd be sore.

But I thought you should know... what I tried to do for you.

Whatever you did, it didn't work, did it?

Look at me!

My skin's so thin... so raw... the *slightest touch* and I *bleed!*

That's why I tried to make a deal.

I thought maybe I could convince them to cure you.

You idiot! I was cursed because I refused to give you to the demons.

I sacrificed *everything* so you could keep your soul.

And what do you do?

You sell your soul anyway!

I should have just let the demons have you in the First place!

Deidra--your tears.

They're making you--

My tears aren't doing anything to me, Pauly!

It's you! You did this!

Don't you give a damn about what I did for you?

All things considered, I probably **deserved** that.

Not because I tried to play Pauly for a chump.

But I should've guessed that the Verlochin were probably offering Pauly the same deal they offered me.

They tried to convince both of us to cheat the other.

And we fell for it.

Pauly I can understand. He's never been too smart when it came to demons.

But me... I ought to have **known better**.

They knew just what to promise me.

They knew I couldn't care less about my soul.

But if they could tell me about my--

You know, Eddie.

When it comes to crawling out of the gutter...

117

...you're a regular *artiste*.

Well, Tony, you know what they say.

Practice makes perfect.

Boy, somebody sure serenaded you with some *chin music*, huh?

You look like you just went ten rounds with a prizefighter...

...maybe even that brother of--

I don't have the key, Tony.

Yeah, I kinda figured from the looks of you.

Who jumped you?

I didn't get a good look.

They hit me from behind.

Well...

...that's just *unsportsmanlike*.

And just when I was gonna bring it to Big Al's doorstep, too.

Right.

Of course, you were.

You're a *square gee*, after all.

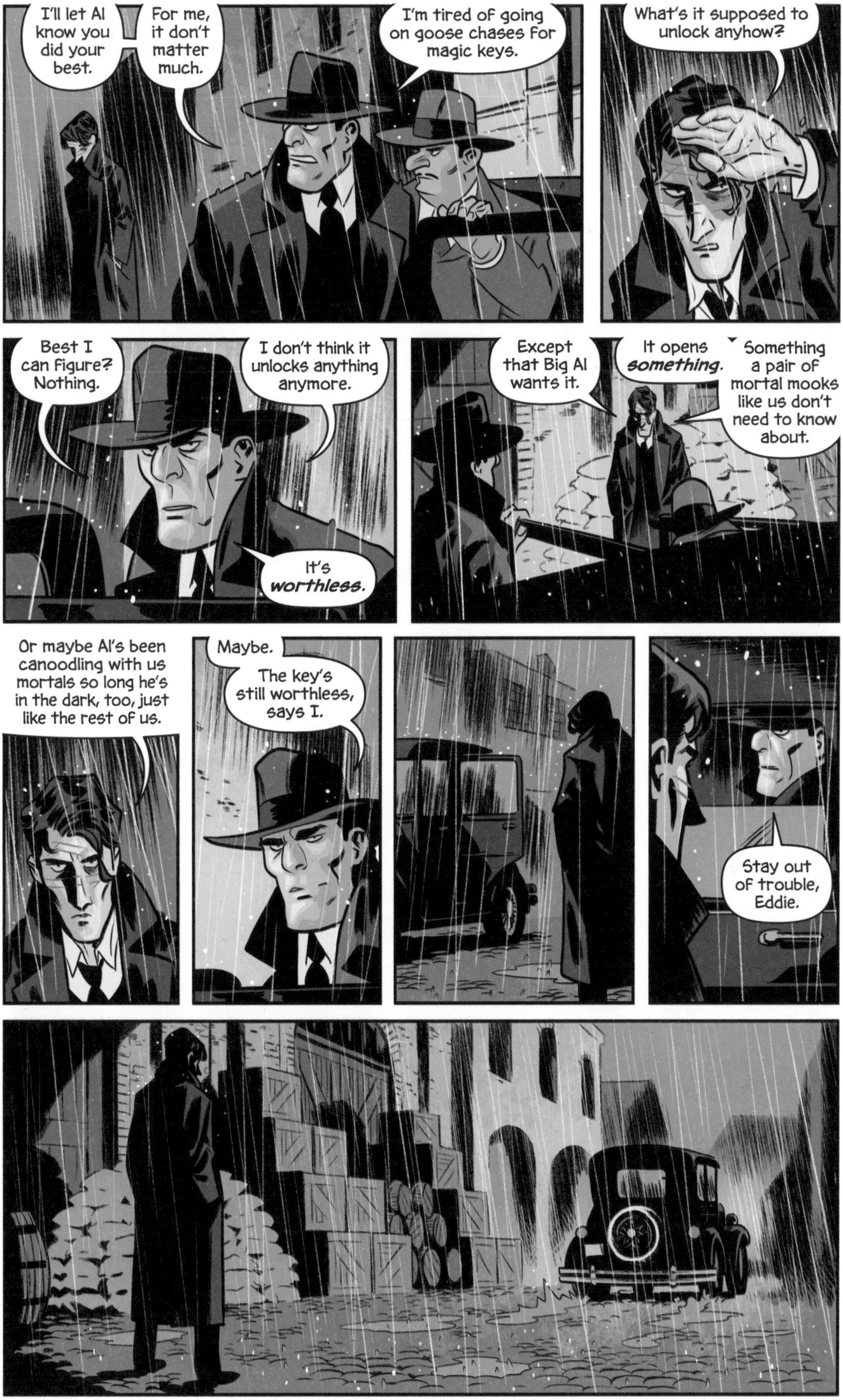
I'll let Al know you did your best.
For me, it don't matter much.
I'm tired of going on goose chases for magic keys.
What's it supposed to unlock anyhow?
Best I can figure? Nothing.
I don't think it unlocks anything anymore.
It's *worthless*.
Except that Big Al wants it.
It opens *something*.
Something a pair of mortal mooks like us don't need to know about.
Or maybe Al's been canoodling with us mortals so long he's in the dark, too, just like the rest of us.
Maybe.
The key's still worthless, says I.
Stay out of trouble, Eddie.

The chances that I've beaten Deidra and Pauly back here are slim.

So why even bother?

Call it *curiosity*.

The *morbid* kind.

CRE EEEAAK

Or maybe I just want the Verlochin to know I tried.

Who's the *goddamned Fetch* now?

Ah, Eddie. Come in, come in.

We've been *expecting* you.

Yeah, I figured the way your spook house door creaked open as I walked up.

Seems to do that a lot.

Maybe we're *always* expecting you.

I see you got what you wanted.

Yes, yes.

It's with us now... where it belongs.

It's quite a piece of *infernal history*, you know.

History.

Deidra and Pauly-- It was a fair bargain.

We *all* got what we wanted.

Except for you, Eddie.

I've got what I need to get by.

But you wanted to serve us, didn't you?

That shows *loyalty*. And loyalty should be *rewarded*.

Let me tell you about your *mother*... and how you can see her once more.

But--Pauly--you haven't even told me where you're taking me yet!

Does it matter, babe?

Me and you, we're getting far from this town... far from these demons.

I feel bad about how we--

We did what we need to do.

End of that story.

But not the end of ours.

You really came through, Pauly.

I shouldn't have doubted you.

That's all behind us now.

Your carriage awaits!

Driver--

H-hey!

Hey now!

We got no beef with you!

It's the Verlochin-- they've got that key of yours.

It's not my key.

BLAM!

BLAM!

Eddie--

We owe you an apology, I suppose.

You don't owe me anything.

Looks like you all still have your curses.

Guess Deidra didn't hold up her end of the bargain.

She lived among us all that time.

She was one of us.

But she just left us the way she did.

You get everything taken from you, you might turn *desperate*.

You turn desperate, you might turn *mean*.

You want to make it up to me?

Pay my tab, why don't ya, Goldy?

I don't know if--

Pull a *tooth* if you have to.

Nothing comes for free.

I learned that lesson a long time ago.

And what the Verlochin told me...

...there's no way that piece of information doesn't come with a *hefty price*.

Only real question, though...

...is how many other people I'm gonna recruit to help me carry the tab.

Mom.

I'm coming for you.

Do you think he *believes?*

Oh, yes.

Eddie is cursed, has been since the day he was born.

But he still clings to hope.

The key--

He thinks it is significant, yes.

No doubt, he'll try to puzzle out what it unlocks.

I thought he was smarter than that.

Be thankful he is not.

If he was, he might somehow learn that this is just one of *many* keys.

One of many that will be used, yes.

Used to usher our kind back to *greatness.*

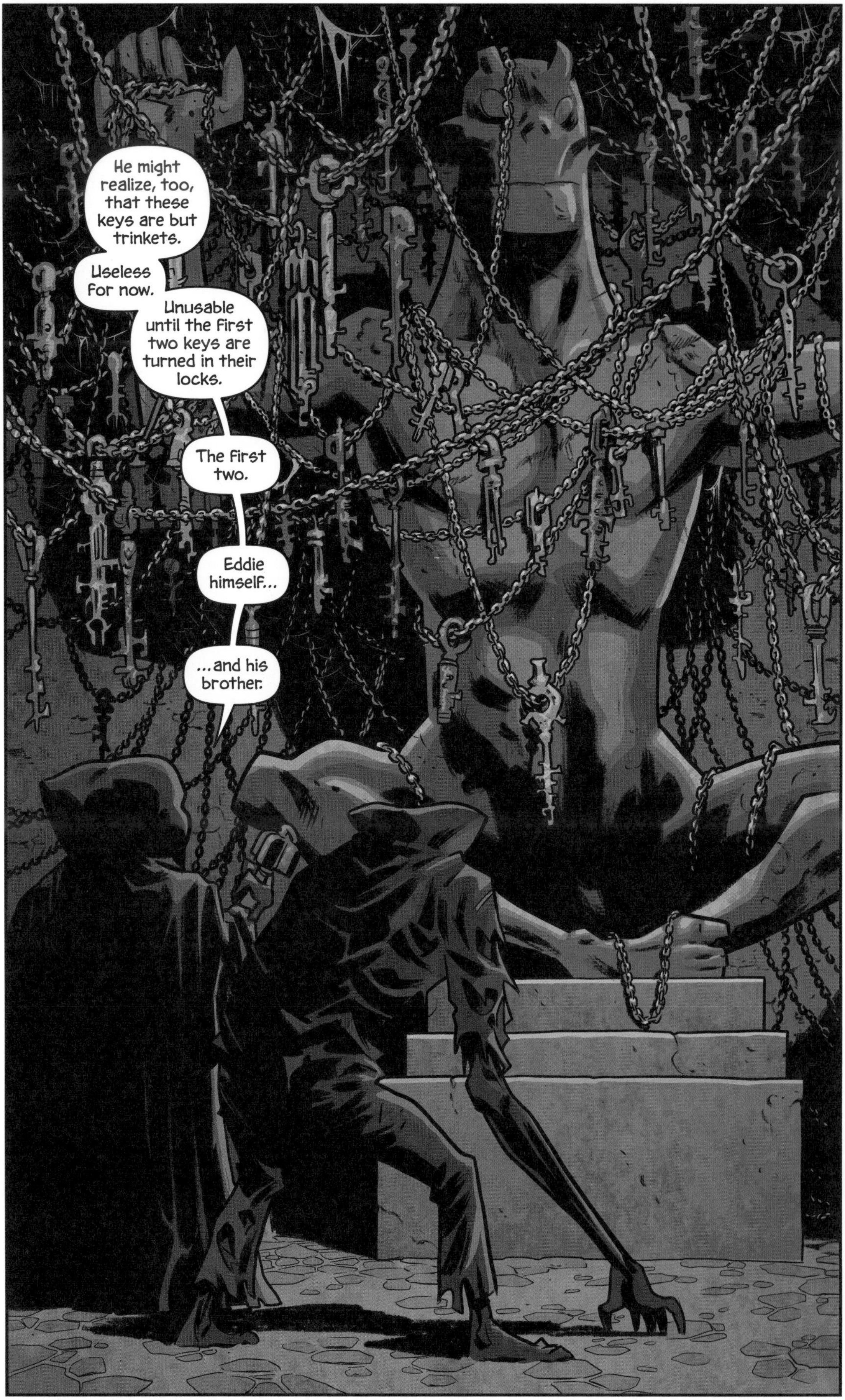
He might realize, too, that these keys are but trinkets.
Useless for now.
Unusable until the first two keys are turned in their locks.
The first two.
Eddie himself...
...and his brother.

THE DAMNED

VOLUME 2, "ILL-GOTTEN"

COVER ARCHIVE

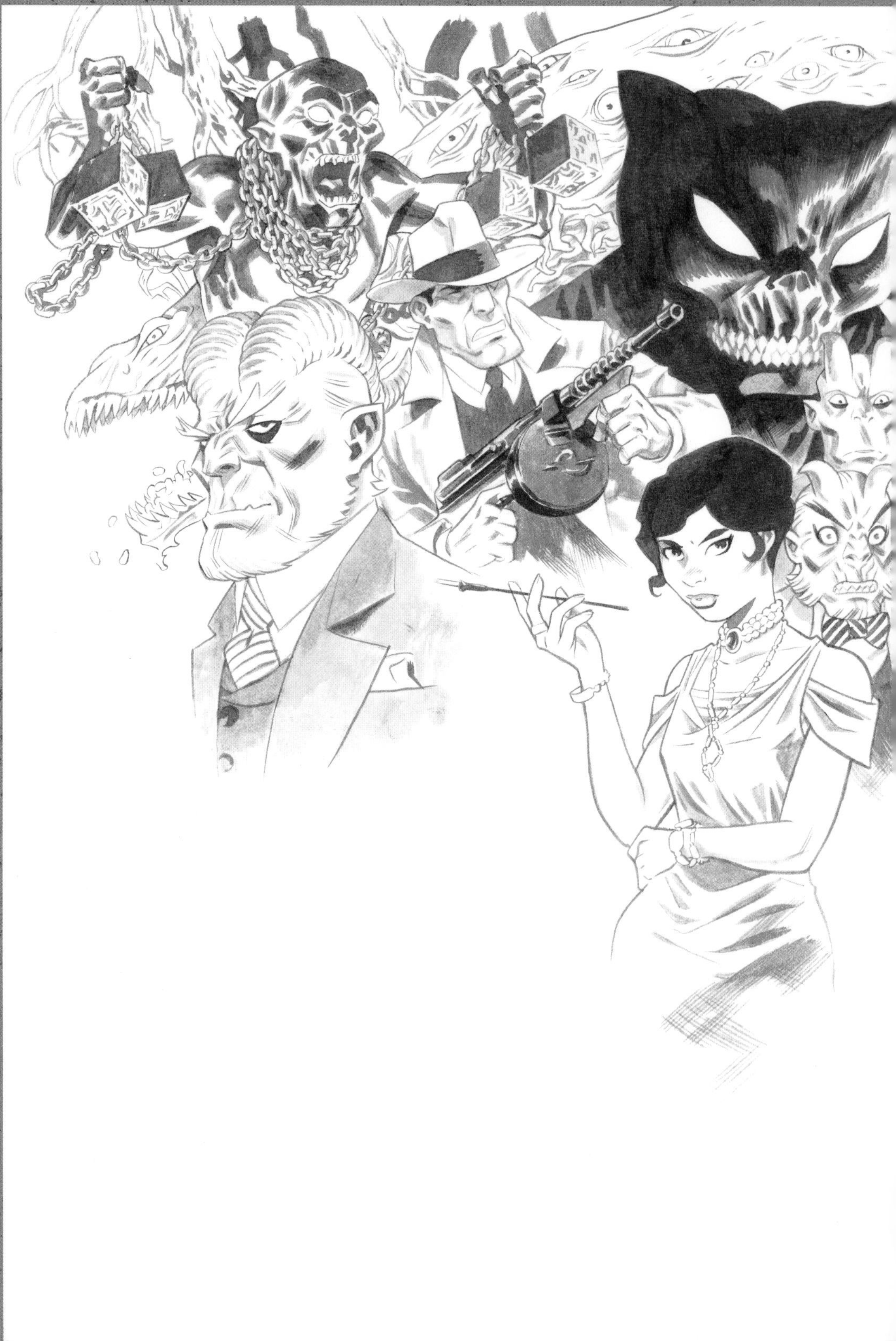

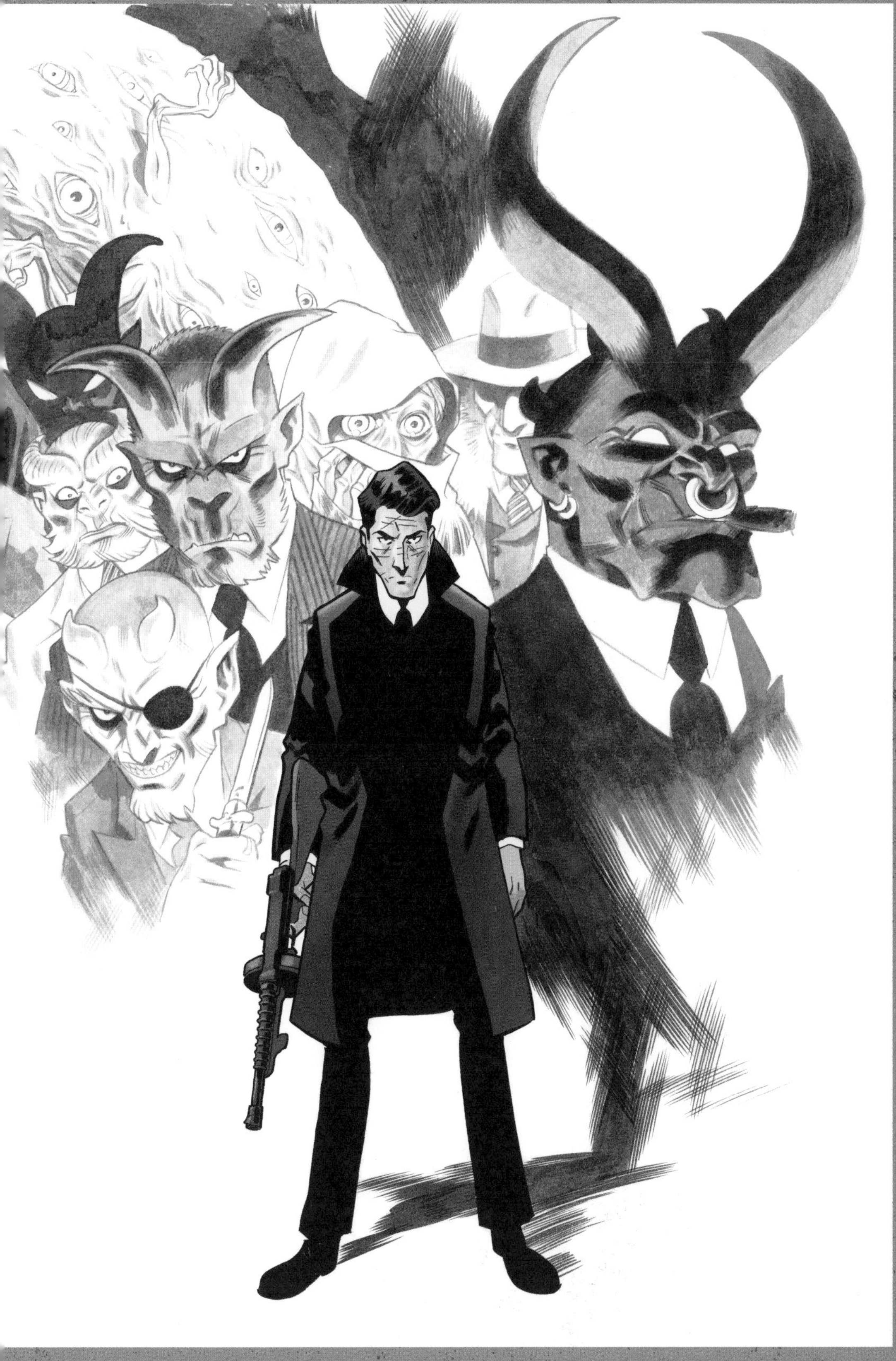

ISSUE #1 COVER

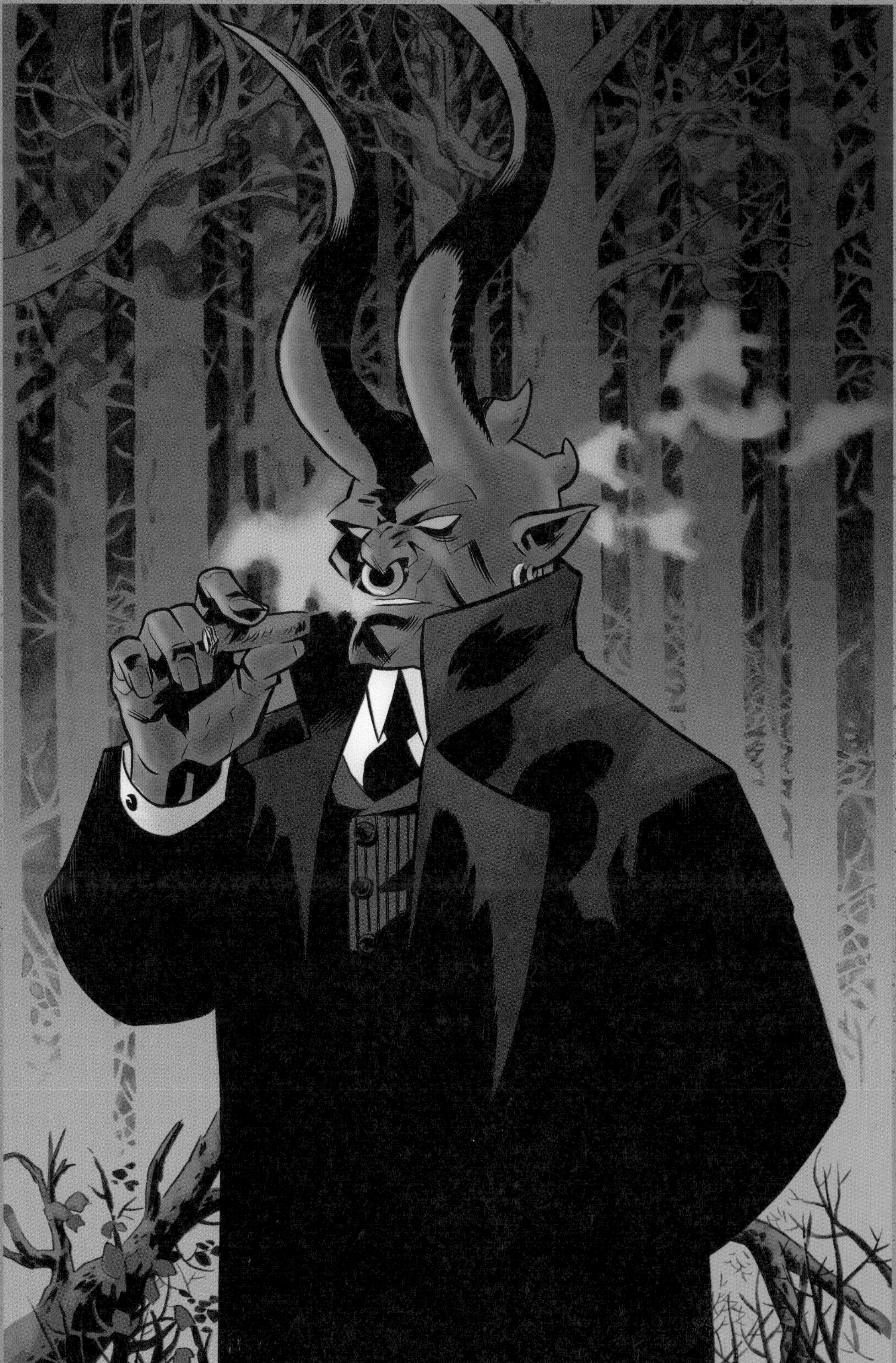

ISSUE #2 COVER

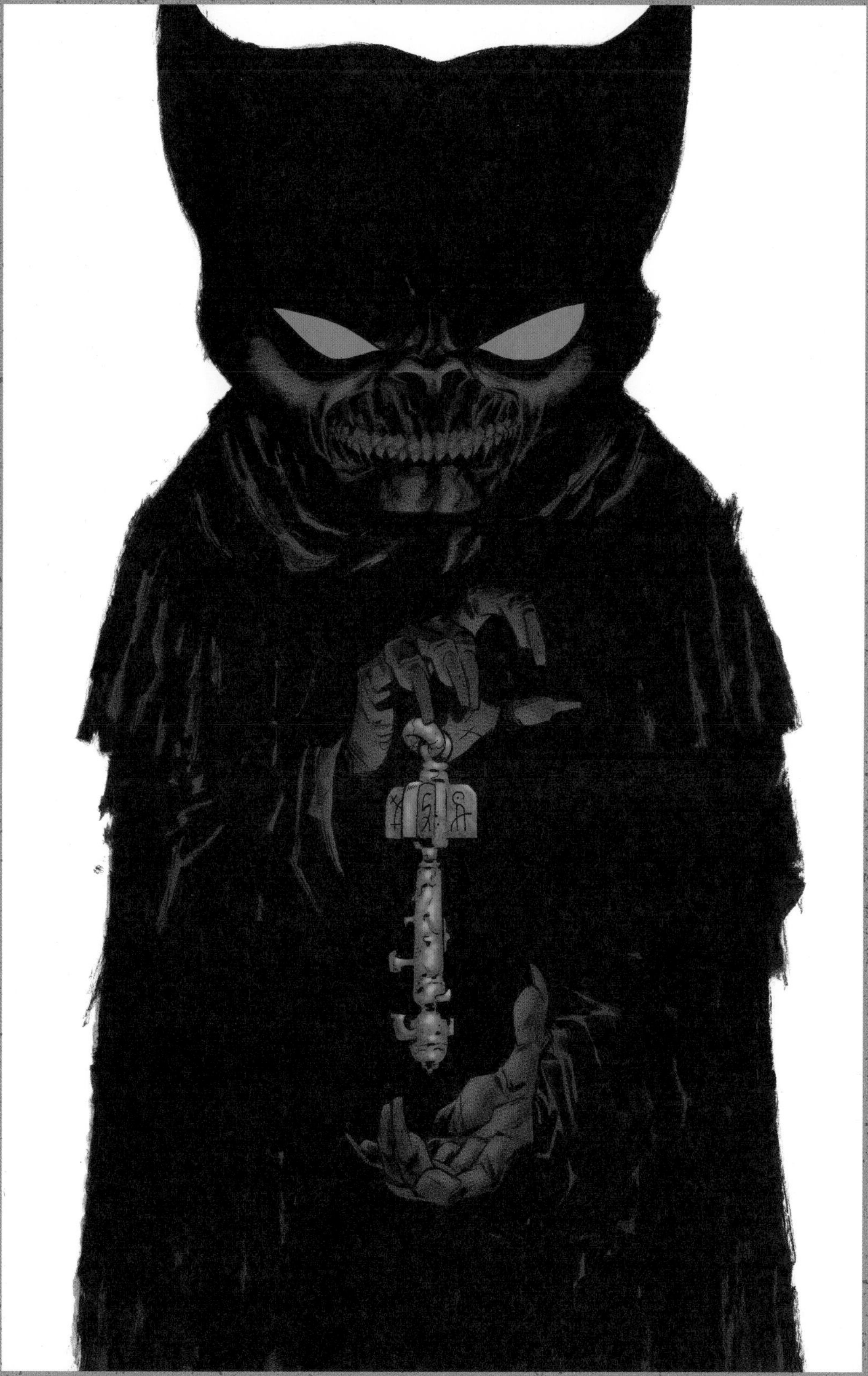

ISSUE #3 COVER

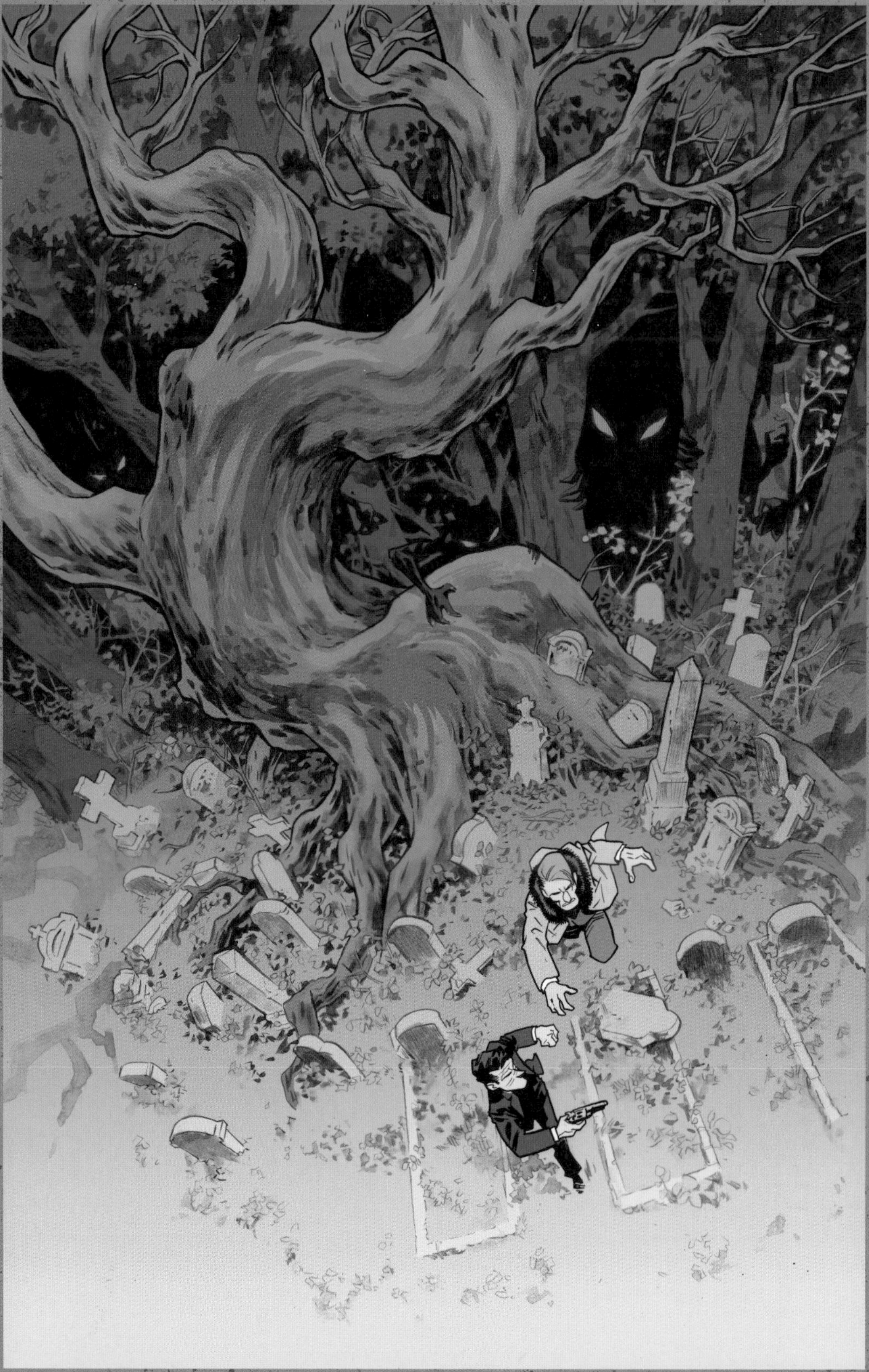

ISSUE #4 COVER

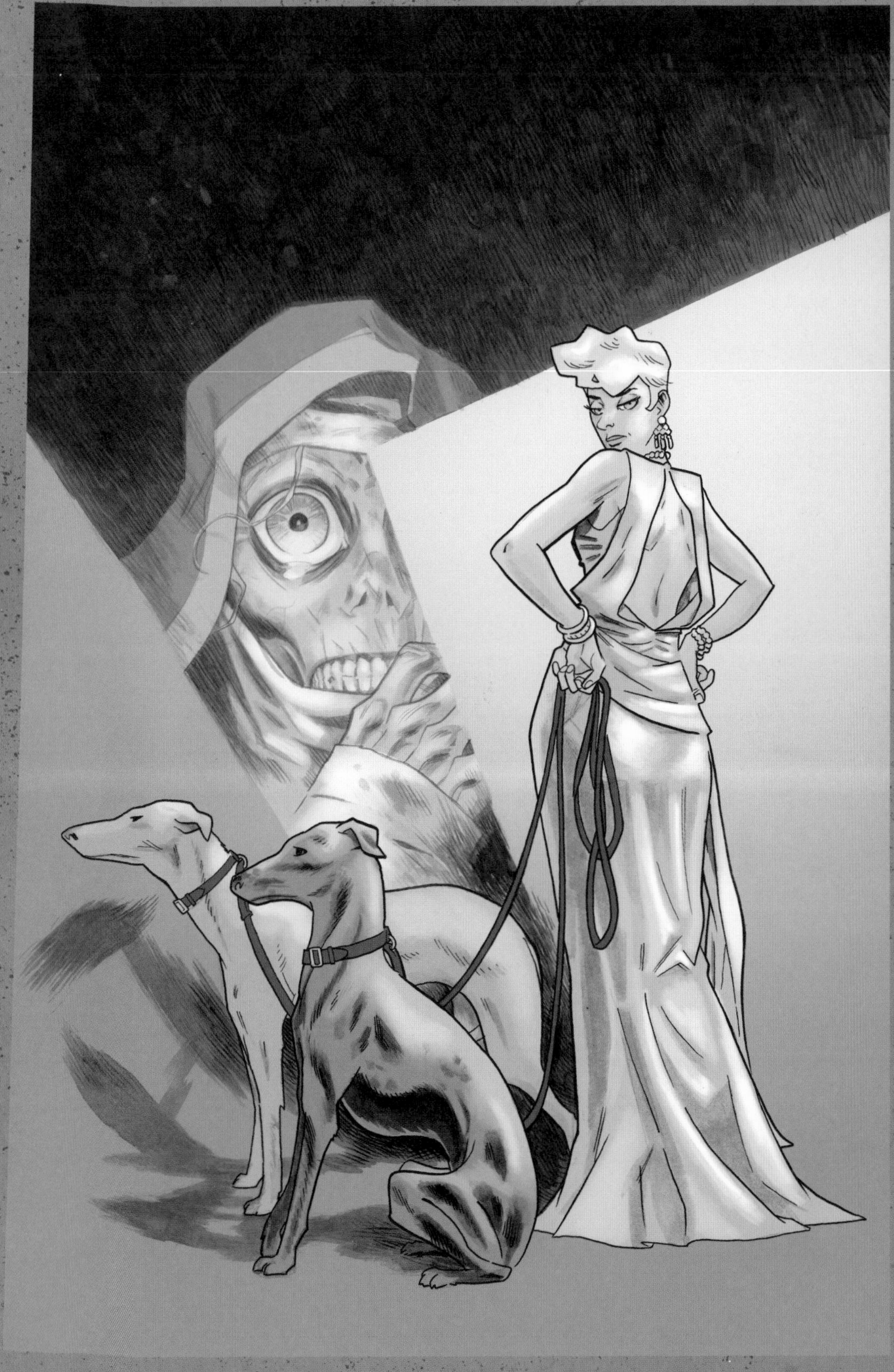

ISSUE #5 COVER

CULLEN BUNN is the writer of comic books such *The Sixth Gun*, *Helheim*, and *The Tooth* for Oni Press. He has also written titles including *Harrow County* (Dark Horse), *Uncanny X-Men*, and *Deadpool and The Mercs For Money* (Marvel).

Cullen claims to have worked as an Alien Autopsy Specialist, Rodeo Clown, Pro Wrestling Manager, and Sasquatch Wrangler. He has fought for his life against mountain lions and performed on stage as the World's Youngest Hypnotist. Buy him a drink sometime, and he'll tell you all about it.

cullenbunn.com · Twitter: @cullenbunn

BRIAN HURTT is an artist/writer who has spent most of his career working on collaborative creator-owned projects. His first such collaboration was in 2006 when Brian teamed with writer Cullen Bunn to create the Prohibition-era, monster-noir, cult classic, *The Damned*. A few years later the two teamed up again to create *The Sixth Gun*—a weird-west, epic supernatural fantasy. Brian also contributes to the popular webcomic *Table Titans*, in which he is the writer and artist of the stories "Whispers of Dragons" and "Road to Embers."

Brian lives and works in St. Louis, Missouri.

Brihurtt.com · Twitter: @brihurtt
Instagram: @brihurtt · tabletitans.com

BILL CRABTREE'S career as a colorist began in 2003 with the launch of Image Comics' *Invincible* and *Firebreather*. He was nominated for a Harvey Award for his work on *Invincible*, and he went on to color the first 50 issues of what would become a flagship Image Comics title. He continues to color *Firebreather*, which was recently made into a feature film on Cartoon Network, *Godland*, and *Jack Staff*.

Perhaps the highlight of his comics career, his role as colorist on the Oni Press series *The Sixth Gun* began with issue 6, and has since been described as "like Christmas morning, but with guns."

@crabtree_bill